Financial Growth

Financial Growth

The Impact of Trading in India

Rafeal Mechlore

Leader Enterprises

CONTENTS

INDEX

Introduction

Introduction

Few factors have been as transformative to India's economic and social growth as the complex world of trading has been. This complicated world has played a significant role in India's great tapestry. The book "Financial Growth: The Impact of Trading in India" takes the reader on an exciting adventure to discover the significant impact that trading in all of its guises has had on the development of India over the course of its long and eventful history. Trading has grown as a dynamic and ubiquitous force that influences not just the economic landscape of the nation, but also the social fabric and cultural character of the country, going beyond the teeming bazaars of ancient civilizations and the vibrant marketplaces of contemporary India.

Trading is more than just a transactional activity; rather, it is a fundamental catalyst that accelerates India's economic progress, generates job opportunities, empowers individuals and communities, and helps foster a sense of economic inclusion. It transcends the physical locations of marketplaces and stock exchanges to penetrate every part of Indian life, from the lowly street seller haggling over pricing to the experienced stock trader navigating the complexities of the financial markets. This book goes deeply into the complex network of trading, investigating its multidimensional impact on India's financial development as well as the tremendous promise it has for the future of the nation.

The historical development of trade in India can be better comprehended with the help of the information contained in this book. The development of trade is a reflection of India's own progression, from its ancient origins, which are firmly ingrained in the cultural practices of the nation, to the emergence of formal marketplaces and the digital trading platforms of the modern period. We discuss some of the most important turning points in the history of trade in India. These turning points not only shed light on the changes that have occurred in the economic climate, but they also demonstrate the dynamic interplay that exists between trading practices and the socio-cultural ethos of the country.

The critical function that commerce plays in the expansion of India's economy is going to be a primary focus of this investigation. This book takes an in-depth look at the crucial role that trading plays in India's Gross Domestic Product (GDP), as well as the ways in which it encourages entrepreneurialism, facilitates the production of capital, and opens the door to investment opportunities. The stock markets, which are the principal vehicles for trading, are investigated in depth, shedding light on the vital role that stock markets play in corporate financing, initial public offers (IPOs), and the growth of businesses.

Case studies and real-life examples highlight how trading in India has been essential in enabling both huge corporations and small-scale entrepreneurs, leaving an indelible mark on the country's economic landscape in the process.

This book devotes a significant amount of attention to the connection between commercial exchange and broadening people's access to financial services. It sheds light on how trade might broaden access to financial markets, clearing the path for rural and underprivileged groups to get involved. Trading has the potential to dramatically reduce income inequality and enhance financial stability for a larger cross-section of the population if it can make the financial system more accessible and inclusive.

As we travel further, we will investigate how the effects of international trade go beyond national boundaries. It investigates the dynamic relationship that exists between domestic and international trade, illuminating the ways in which trading dynamics impact India's international trade activities, such as import-export transactions, trade agreements, and currency exchanges. Trading has become an increasingly important part of India's relationship with the rest of the world as the country continues to strengthen its place in the global economy.

In addition to this, the author does not shy away from discussing the tremendous impact that technological advancement and creative thinking have had on the business scene. In this article, we explore the technical developments, such as algorithmic trading, blockchain, and cryptocurrencies, that have completely altered the trading scene in India. This book offers a look into the future of trading technology and discusses the potential effects that it could have on India's financial markets.

There is no way to have a comprehensive conversation about trading without first admitting the difficulties and dangers it entails. We discuss the impact of global economic events, as well as market volatility, risk management, regulatory impediments, and ethical considerations. It offers a complete perspective on the complexity that are inherent to trading and places an emphasis on the requirement for sensible risk management and ethical procedures in order to guarantee the viability of the trading ecosystem.

The influence of trading extends much deeper, playing a role in the evolution of society. We investigate the role that trading plays in India's progress toward reaching the Sustainable Development Goals, specifically with regard to infrastructure projects, educational and professional development, and charitable giving. The book illustrates the interconnectivity between trade and broader social wellbeing, illustrating how this economic power may be exploited for the greater good. The interconnectedness between trading and broader societal welfare is highlighted throughout the book.

As we come to the close of our investigation, we will provide some insights into potential future developments and patterns. The business landscape in India is constantly shifting, which brings with it a wide range of opportunities and obstacles. This book offers helpful ideas and insights that will assist the reader in navigating this ever-changing terrain and getting ready for the future.

The book "Financial Growth: The Impact of Trading in India" is a tribute to the on-going significance of trading in molding the destiny of the nation in a country where trading has been woven into the fabric of everyday life for millennia. This book was written in India, a country where trading has been woven into the fabric of daily life for millennia. It provides a comprehensive understanding of the delicate relationship between financial markets, economic development, and societal advancement, serving as a crucial guide for economists, policymakers, entrepreneurs, and anyone intrigued by India's economic path. This book highlights the revolutionary force of trading as well as its lasting impact on India's financial progress, leaving an indelible mark on the collective path of the nation.

1. **The Significance of Trading**

    The act of trading goods and services is one of the most fundamental human activities and has been instrumental in the evolution of human communities for many years. Trading is a multi-faceted behavior that involves the exchange of products, services, or financial assets; it also has major implications for the economy, culture, and society. Throughout the course of this investigation, we will look into the significance of trading and the ways in which it has influenced the progression of human history, from the earliest forms of bartering to the most sophisticated financial markets.

    The Origins of Commerce Throughout History

    Since the beginning of civilization, people have been exchanging goods and services with one another. Barter was the primary method that communities used to obtain commodities and services before the development of contemporary monetary systems. The practice of exchanging one good or service for another, such as swapping crops for animals or equipment for textiles, is an example of bartering. Individuals were able to acquire resources they did not have while simultaneously getting rid of stuff they had in excess because to this straightfor-ward procedure. The historical relevance of trading was further demonstrated by the establishment of several trade routes, such as the Silk Road and the Spice Trade. These trade routes connected previously isolated cultures and made it possible for the exchange of unusual items.

    Significance to the Economy:

    The economic impact of trading is one of the characteristics of its significance that is most readily visible. Trading is one of the primary engines that propel economic expansion and wealth. It makes the efficient allocation of resources possible, enabling producers to specialize in what they do best and trade their surplus for commodities that they require. The increased productivity resulting from this specialization and interchange contributes to the expansion of the economy as a whole. Competition, innovation, and the creation of new jobs are all stimulated by a robust ecology for commerce, which is important for an economy to be in good condition.

Particularly significant to the expansion of the economy is the activity of trading goods across international borders. It enables nations to capitalize on their comparative advantages by exporting the goods at which they excel and importing those goods which they are unable to produce as efficiently as their competitors. This not only makes a wider selection of products accessible to customers, but it also gives them access to products that may not be sold in their immediate area. It encourages peaceful coexistence as well as diplomatic ties, which in turn helps to build global interdependence.

Importance to Social and Cultural Traditions:

The importance of commerce to both society and culture cannot be overstated. It has been a driving force behind the exchange of other civilizations' ideas, technologies, and perspectives. The exchange of people and things along trade routes has resulted in the cross-fertilization of civilizations, which has had an effect on aspects of society such as art, language, religion, and norms of behavior. The diversity of cultures found in many areas may be traced back hundreds of years to the movement of people along with cultural and economic interchange.

In addition, the growth and collapse of civilizations has been partially attributed to the rise and

fall of trading. In the past, prosperous empires have frequently been linked to thriving trade routes. One example of this is the Roman Empire, which dominated vital trading routes during antiquity. On the other hand, the disappearance of important trade routes is frequently a precursor to the fall of one empire and the development of a new world power. Throughout the course of history, the shifting currents of trade have been a significant factor in shaping the geopolitical dynamics.

Importance from a Financial Standpoint:

Trading now has a presence in the realm of finance thanks to the advancements made in modern times. The trading of many types of financial assets, including stocks, bonds, currencies, and commodities, has centralized itself in the world's financial markets. These markets are extremely important in terms of both the distribution of money and the establishment of pricing for various financial products.

For instance, by participation in the stock market, businesses are able to increase their financial resources by selling shares to the general public. Investors are given the opportunity to buy and sell these shares, which increases liquidity and encourages investment activity.

Trading in financial markets, with its intricate web of instruments and tactics, has evolved into its own independent area of specialization. Traders profit from changes in market conditions by analyzing market data, deciding how to allocate their investments, and carrying out trades. When it comes to investing, managing wealth, and planning for retirement, the financial markets are extremely important. They create a dynamic financial ecosystem by connecting investors and borrowers with opportunities and connecting borrowers with lenders.

Recent Developments in Technology:

The importance of business transactions has been significantly bolstered as a result of developments in technology. Electronic trading platforms have mostly succeeded traditional trading floors in the modern period, making it simpler and more expedient to carry out financial transactions. The financial markets have been transformed by algorithmic trading, which is driven by complicated computer algorithms. This has made it possible to engage in high-frequency trading and quantitative analysis.

Trading is another industry that has been democratized by digital technologies. Individual investors are now able to join in financial markets that were previously mostly open to institutional investors because to the proliferation of online brokerage platforms. The democratization of technology has resulted in an increase in the number of chances for individuals to amass wealth and make preparations for their financial futures.

Difficulties and Potential Dangers:

Although there are many advantages to trading, it is not without its share of difficulties and

dangers. For example, market volatility can cause considerable price movements, which can result in monetary losses for both traders and investors. Trading requires careful attention to risk management in order to reduce the likelihood of financial loss.

Another big worry, particularly in the financial markets, is the difficulty of meeting regulatory requirements. The establishment of rules and checks and balances by regulatory agencies is done with the goal of protecting the markets' honesty and reliability. A trusting and stable market requires strict adherence to these standards, which are crucial to that goal.

Concerns of a moral nature, such as those involving insider trading, market manipulation, and fraud, are also common in the trading industry.

These unethical acts have the potential to destroy investor confidence and damage the integrity of the market. For this reason, a healthy trading environment requires both ethical behavior and a strict adherence to the regulations that govern the market.

The Path Ahead for Business:

Because of the growing interconnectedness of the world, the significance of commerce is constantly shifting in new directions. The current state of the world's financial system is being disrupted by technological developments such as blockchain and cryptocurrency. The use of these innovations has the potential to broaden access to financial markets, as well as boost transparency and decrease fraud. There is a possibility that new asset classes and market structures may become a part of the future of trading. These developments will reflect the shifting requirements and preferences of traders and investors.

The act of trade is an activity that has significant relevance not only economically, but also socially, culturally, and financially. It has been a primary factor in the expansion of economies, the sharing of cultural traditions, and the development and demise of civilizations. The advent of the modern age witnessed the development of trading into financial markets, with technology playing a pivotal role in this transformation. It is impossible to overstate the significance of commerce as a constant engine of development, notwithstanding the difficulties and dangers normally connected with it. When we look to the future, we may expect that trade will continue to adapt and develop, bringing about interesting and novel changes in the global economy and financial markets.

2. **Historical Context of Trading in India**

It is a rich tapestry that extends back millennia, and it reflects the nation's deep-rooted economic and cultural linkages to the rest of the world. The history of trading in India dates back to those times. India has had a significant impact on international commerce ever since ancient times, leaving a legacy that stretches from the civilization that flourished in the Indus Valley to the thriving market of the current period. In this investigation, we dive into the historical context of commerce in India. More specifically, we track the growth of trading methods, as well as the influence of international trade routes and the cultural impact of trading on the subcontinent.

Roots in Early Commercial Activity:

Trading customs in India may be traced all the way back to the Indus Valley civilization, which was one of the earliest urban centers in the world. These customs date back thousands of years. The people who lived in the Indus Valley participated in both local and long-distance commerce. They traded commodities like textiles, pottery, and precious metals with the people who lived in other places. The unearthing of objects and seals from this time period provides evidence that a sophisticated commercial network existed at this time.

The Vedic period, which lasted from 1500 BCE to 500 BCE, was the time when the Indus Valley civilization changed into a more agricultural society. During this historical period, commerce continued to play an essential role in Indian civilization. The Rigveda is one of the first sacred scriptures associated with Hinduism. Within its pages, references to trade caravans, merchants, and the buying and selling of products are made as everyday occurrences.

Empire of the Mauryans :

The Mauryan Empire, which lasted roughly 322–185 BCE, was one of the earliest empires to have a significant impact on the history of trade in India. During the reign of Emperor Ashoka, India's commercial ties reached as far as Greece, Persia, and even parts of the eastern Mediterranean. During this time period, a centralized currency system was put into place, along with the building of roads and other infrastructure to facilitate trade.

The Spice Route and the Silk Road:

The historical significance of India's role in the Silk Road and the Spice Trade is another example of the country's importance to international commerce. The Silk Road was an extensive network of trade routes that connected East and West, and it made it easier for people to trade products, ideas, and civilizations with one another. Spices, textiles, and diamonds were some of the most highly prized goods that were traded along the southern branch of the Silk Road, and India played an important role as a hub along this route. Traders from all over the world traveled to India's Malabar Coast to take part in the Spice Trade, which was characterized by bustling marketplaces. It was common practice in Europe and the Middle East to pay a high price for Indian spices such as black pepper, cardamom, and cinnamon.

Trade in the Middle Ages and Arab Merchants:

During the medieval period, India's trading links increased, and powerful trading societies such as the Cholas and the Pallavas dominated the marine trade routes. This contributed to India's economic growth. Arab merchants played a vital part in the economic operations that took place in India and established trading towns along the western coast of the country. They made it easier for people to trade items such as textiles, spices, and jewels, which strengthened the political, economic, and cultural relations between India and the Arab world.

Empire of the Mughals :

The Mughal Empire, which lasted from 1526 until 1857, was a high point in the historical significance of trade in India. The empire was a flourishing commercial hub that merchants from all over the world flocked to because of its favorable conditions for doing business. The Mughals were responsible for the development of a monetary system, the standardization of currency, and the construction of infrastructure to facilitate trade, including the Grand Trunk Road. During this time period, India's textile industry was booming, and its wares were being shipped all over the world, including to Europe, Persia, and Southeast Asia.

The artistic and cultural interchange that took place during this century is represented by the Mughal Empire's cultural synthesis as well as its architectural marvels, such as the Red Fort in Delhi and the Taj Mahal in Agra.

Colonialism across Europe and the British Raj in India:
When European colonial forces first established themselves in India, the historical framework of the country's commercial activity underwent a considerable shift. Along the coast of India, European powers such as the Portuguese, Dutch, French, and British erected trading posts and forts, gradually increasing their spheres of influence. In particular, the British East India Company had a significant impact on the development of trade in India during the course of its history.

India's economy grew highly interwoven into the system of international commerce while it was still under British colonial authority. While the British were taking advantage of India's natural resources, they also modernized the country's infrastructure by constructing railways, telegraph lines, and ports, which increased India's capacity for international trade. However, the economic and social effects of British colonialism were complicated due to the fact that it resulted in the exploitation of the Indian economy and the exhaustion of the country's resources.

Liberation with Political and Economic Changes:
The fight for independence from British colonial control in India resulted in a refocused attention on the importance of self-sufficiency and economic autonomy. India became an independent nation in 1947, and almost immediately began a process of economic modernization and advancement. The goal of achieving economic self-sufficiency drove the creation of economic policies such as import substitution and state control over important industries. Additionally, India made strenuous efforts to cultivate diplomatic connections and business alliances with nations located all over the world.

Globalization and the Contemporary Era:
India has transformed into a major economic player on the world stage in the modern era. The Indian economy became more accessible to international commerce and investment when it underwent liberalization in the 1990s. In particular, the information technology (IT) and software services sector has been an essential contributor to the expansion of India's economy as well as its participation in international trade. The rise of the nation to prominence as a center for the provision of services related to information technology has contributed to an increase in the significance of its commercial role.

Influence on Culture:
The historical setting of trading in India has permanently imprinted itself on the culture and identity of the nation. Indian civilization and its trading partners have contributed to the development of a diverse and pluralistic culture by exchanging ideas, languages, religious beliefs, and artistic practices. This cultural interchange is visible in several aspects of Indian society, such as architecture, cuisine, clothes, and religious rituals, all of which bear the impact of different

trading partners over the course of several centuries.

The long-standing relevance of India as a trading nation in the global economy is demonstrated by the historical setting of the country's commercial activity. From the ancient civilization of the Indus Valley to the worldwide marketplace of the 21st century, India's trading history has developed and changed, leaving behind a significant imprint on the country's socioeconomic and cultural fabric. The complex history of commerce in India is influenced by a number of factors, including the country's long-standing linkages to international trade routes, the legacy of its colonial past, and the present-day era of economic liberalization. The nation's long trading tradition will continue to be an essential component of both its past and its future, as it plays an increasingly important role in the economy of the world as a whole.

3. **Purpose and Scope of the Book**

The book "Financial Growth: The Impact of Trading in India" is an investigation into the complex nature of the trading industry as it pertains to the Indian setting. In this chapter, we go deeper into the purpose and scope of the book, elaborating on its goals, the questions it aims to answer, and the subjects it discusses in greater detail.

1. Comprehending the Importance of Commercial Transactions
   This book's major objective is to provide a detailed analysis of the significance of trading within the context of Indian history. Throughout the entirety of India's history, commerce has been an essential driver of the country's socioeconomic, cultural, and political development. Our goal is to shed light on the ways in which this time-honored tradition has developed throughout the centuries, the effects it has had on various elements of Indian culture, and the role it has played in defining the future of the nation.

2. Investigating the Predecessors in History:
   One of the primary goals of the book is to provide readers a comprehensive grasp of the historical setting of trade in India, and this is one of its core focuses. We shall investigate India's historical commercial origins, which helped to pave the way for the country's prominent position in the international trading network. The book will look into how trade practices have evolved over time, from the ancient barter system to the modern financial markets. This will demonstrate the ever-present significance of trading throughout history.

3. The Impact on the Economy and Growth:
   Our goal is to shed light on the economic significance of doing business in India. Trading is one of the most important factors contributing to economic expansion, and in this section, we will investigate the ways in which it makes resource allocation more effective, promotes specialization, and fosters innovation. In addition to this, the book will provide light on how the effects of trading have

had an affect on India's Gross Domestic Product (GDP), job generation, and investment prospects.

4. Global Interactions and the Role of International Trade:
   The history of India's trade is intricately entwined with its interactions with the rest of the world. This book will discuss India's position in international trade routes such as the Silk Road and the Spice Trade, as well as how these links shaped India's economic and cultural landscape at the time. We will investigate India's trading interactions with other countries, with a focus on the influence that India's position in the global economy derives from its participation in international commerce.

5. Intercultural Communication and Its Effects on Society:
   Trading has played an important role in the dissemination of culture and the progression of society in India. This book will investigate the role that trading has had in the dissemination of people, ideas, and civilizations throughout history. In this lesson, we are going to investigate the impact that commerce has had on several aspects of culture, including religion, art, and language. Through an analysis of the interrelationships that exist between commercial exchange and broader societal well-being, we will highlight the ways in which commercial exchange contributes to the progress of India's society.

6. The Financial Markets and the Latest Technological Developments:
   Since the dawn of the modern era, India's financial markets have developed into one of the country's most important centers for commercial activity. The relevance of trading in financial markets, such as stock exchanges and currency markets, will be investigated in depth throughout this book. We will address the influence that recent technology developments in trade, such as blockchain and algorithmic trading, have had on the current state of the financial landscape.

7. Obstacles, dangers, and ethical issues to consider:
   Trading comes with a number of inherent difficulties and dangers. The book will discuss topics such as the obstacles posed by regulatory bodies, risk management, and volatile market conditions. The relevance of ethical behavior and regulatory compliance in the trading sector will be emphasized as we delve into ethical challenges such as insider trading and market manipulation.

8. The Prospects for Business in the Future:
   In this section, we will discuss the prospects for business in India in the future. The financial markets are in a state of perpetual flux, and this book will analyze the latest developments in terms of trends, technologies, and opportunities. Our goal is to provide insightful ideas that will assist you in navigating this ever-changing terrain and becoming ready for the future.

9. Promoting an Integrative and Holistic Approach:
   The author made a conscious decision to cover a wide range of topics in this work, including the historical, economic, cultural, social, and technological

elements of trading. The purpose of this article is to persuade readers to adopt a holistic perspective on the significance of trading in India, acknowledging the myriad ways in which it has impacted India's history, both recent and more recent, as well as its future.

10. The Intended Readership:

This book is written with a wide range of readers in mind. It will be of interest to economists, policymakers, entrepreneurs, history fans, history enthusiasts, traders, investors, and anybody wondering about the deep relationship between trading and India's growth narrative.

The objective of "Financial Growth: The Impact of Trading in India" is to present a full understanding of the historical context of trading in India as well as the far-reaching relevance of this activity. This understanding is the aim and scope of the study. The book will take readers on a journey through the annals of history to discover the trading habits that have defined the nation and will dive into how commerce continues to play an important role in India's economic, cultural, and social environment. We have high hopes that readers will come away with a profound new understanding of the persistent impact that commerce has had and will continue to have on India's past, present, and future.

D. Outline of Chapters

The historical development of trade in India is covered in Chapter 1.

This chapter lays the historical groundwork for the rest of the book by providing a comprehensive survey of the many commercial practices that have existed in India over the course of its history. It begins with the Indus Valley Civilization and continues on into the Vedic period as it investigates the origins of early commercial activity. This article examines the development of trade during the Mauryan Empire and the significance of that development in linking India with the rest of the globe. Following this, the chapter investigates India's important role in the Silk Road and Spice commercial, as well as the impact of commercial patterns prevalent during the middle ages and the participation of Arab merchants. The discussion of the impact of European colonialism and the British Raj, as well as how India's commercial history shaped India's journey to freedom and modern globalization, comes to a head in the final section of the chapter.

The Importance of Trading to the Economic System in Chapter 2.

This chapter focuses on the economic aspect of trading, with an emphasis on the significance of trading as a driver of economic progress in India. It throws light on how trading contributes to the efficient allocation of resources, which eventually stimulates economic progress. It also highlights how specialization and innovation are all products of trading. This chapter examines the impact that trade has on India's Gross Domestic Product (GDP), as well as the prospects for investment and employment development that it presents. Trading's position as a driver of economic expansion will be demonstrated using case studies and examples from the real world to emphasize the significance of trading from an economic standpoint.

The Meaning of Business in an International Setting In Chapter 3.

The reader will be taken on a tour through India's historical and contemporary links with other countries involved in international trade in this chapter. It emphasizes the importance of India's vital role in global trade routes while also highlighting the influence of international trade on the economic and cultural environment of the nation. This chapter investigates India's historical relationships with its commercial partners as well as its position in global trade networks such as the Silk Road and the Spice Trade. In addition to this, it looks into India's trading relationships with a variety of countries, highlighting how India's standing in the global economy has been impacted by its participation in international commerce.

The Effects of Trading on Culture and Society In Chapter 4.

The cultural and social ramifications of trading are the topics that are going to be discussed in this chapter. It investigates the role that commerce has had in fostering the sharing of ideas, cultural practices, and social conventions. The reader will obtain an understanding of the significant impact that trade had on the art, language, and religious beliefs as well as the sociological activities of India. This chapter emphasizes the interrelated nature of commercial activity and larger societal wellbeing, providing an example of how commercial activity contributes to the growth of India's cultural and social institutions.

Financial Markets and Technological Advancements is the topic of Chapter 5.

The reader is given an introduction to the current era of trade in this chapter, with the primary attention being placed on technology improvements and financial markets. This article presents a comprehensive investigation into the function that trading plays in various financial markets, including stock exchanges and currency markets. This chapter also goes into the technology advancements, such as algorithmic trading, blockchain, and cryptocurrencies, that have significantly altered the trading landscape. This provides a glimpse into the future of trading technology and the potential effects that this could have on India's financial markets.

The Obstacles, Dangers, and Ethical Concerns of the Situation in Chapter 6

This chapter discusses the difficulties and dangers that are inherent in the trading industry. It explores topics such as the volatility of the market, risk management, the difficulties posed by regulatory agencies, and ethical considerations such as insider trading and market manipulation. This chapter places a strong emphasis on the importance of ethical behavior and regulatory compliance in the realm of trading, and it provides insights into how these issues might be managed and minimized.

The Crucial Function of Commercial Activity in India's Economic Growth

This chapter examines how trade contributes to India's infrastructure development, education and skill upgrading, philanthropic endeavors, and progress toward the Sustainable Development Goals. The chapter focuses on the larger social impact of trading and examines how trade contributes to these areas. It highlights how the act of trading may act as a catalyst for good change, so making a discernible impact in the lives of individuals as well as in the lives of communities.

Emerging Trends and Future Prospects is the topic of Chapter 8.

The book comes to a close with a chapter that discusses the prospects of business in India in the future. It offers insights into developing trends, opportunities, and problems that the trading landscape is expected to observe in the coming years. These are all things that are likely to occur in the following years. The readers will get helpful pointers for navigating this dynamic and always changing area, which will ensure that they are well-prepared for the future of trading in India.

This extensive book intends to give readers with a well-rounded perspective on the significance of commerce in India, including its historical roots, economic impact, cultural and social influence, and its future prospects. The scope of the book's coverage encompasses all of these aspects: history, economics, culture, and society. When taken as a whole, the chapters contribute to a more complete comprehension of the significant part that commerce has played in the formation of India's history, as well as its present and its future.

The Evolution of Trading in India

Trading is an essential part of human civilization, and the development of commercial exchange is intricately connected to the history of nations and the growth of their economies. India, with its extensive history and long-standing tradition of commerce, provides an intriguing case study of how trading practices have changed over the course of the ages. India's rich legacy and long-standing tradition of trade. The transition from traditional forms of exchange, such as barter, to contemporary financial markets can be seen reflected in the development of trading in India. During this investigation, we will delve into the complex and multifaceted history of trading in India. We will trace its beginnings, key historical landmarks, and its current position in the economy of the world.

1. **An Introduction: The Significance of Commercial Exchanges**
   Before digging into the history of trading in India, it is essential to have an appreciation for the significance of this aspect of the country's economy. Trading involves more than just the basic exchange of things; it is essential to the expansion of the economy, the sharing of cultures, and interaction on a global scale. It has been a significant factor in the making of India's history and is a driving force in the continued growth of the country's economy and society.

2. **Origins in Antiquity: Commercial Interactions in the Indus Valley Civilization**
   In India, commerce dates back to the time of the ancient Indus Valley Civilization, which is where its beginnings may be found. This amazing culture, which dates back to approximately 2500 BCE, was involved in trading on both a local and a long-distance scale. The people who lived in the Indus Valley engaged in trade with people from other regions, exchanging products such as ceramics, textiles, and precious metals. In doing so, they established the groundwork for future commercial operations on the Indian subcontinent.

3. **The Vedic Period: Convergence and Commercial Activity**
   The time period known as the Vedic period, which lasted from about 1500 to 500 BCE, was a pivotal one in the annals of India's history. Even though an agricultural civilization began to take shape during this time, commerce continued to be an essential part of everyday life. The Rigveda is one of the oldest sacred scriptures in the Hindu religion. This chapter examines references to trade caravans, merchants, and the exchange of products that are found throughout the Rigveda.

4. **The Mauryan Empire was a thriving commercial center during its time**
   The Mauryan Empire (about 322–185 BCE), which was ruled by Emperor Ashoka, developed into a prosperous trading hub throughout his administration. The importance of trade in establishing connections between India and other locations, including Greece, Persia, and even the eastern Mediterranean, is examined in this chapter. This chapter sheds light on the breadth of India's trading links during a period in which India was an active participant in international trade.

5. **India's Importance to World Trade in the Era of the Silk Road and the Spice Trade**
   One of the most iconic representations of historical commerce is the Silk Road, which was an immense network of trade routes that connected East and West. Along the southern route of the Silk Road, India played a significant position in the global economic system by virtue of the important role it played along the Silk Road. This chapter examines India's role in the Silk Road and its commerce in spices, textiles, and jewels, all of which were highly sought-after goods in far-off marketplaces. Additionally, the chapter looks at India's involvement in the Silk Road.

6. **Maritime Dominance Achieved Through Medieval Trade and Arab Traders**
   During the medieval period, significant commercial communities in India, such as the Cholas and the Pallavas, helped India to become the dominant player in marine trade. Arab merchants played a vital part in the economic operations that took place in India and established trading towns along the western coast of the country. This chapter examines the role that Arab merchants had in the development of a thriving spice trade along the Malabar Coast of India.

7. **The Mughal Empire was the height of India's commercial significance during this time**
   The Mughal Empire, which ruled India from 1526 to 1857, was responsible for one of the most profitable periods in India's trading history. The Mughals were the ones who first developed a monetary system, standardized coinage, and built the infrastructure necessary to facilitate trade. This chapter takes a look at India's thriving textile industry, which was responsible for the country's sale of textiles to Europe, Persia, and Southeast Asian countries. Additionally, it highlights the

significance of the Mughal Empire's influence on India's cultural and economic landscape.

8. **Colonialism in Europe and the British Raj: The Influence of Colonial Rule on Trade**

The introduction of European colonial powers into India's trading history, especially the Portuguese, Dutch, French, and British, had a profound impact on the development of trade in India. This chapter examines the impact that the British colonial government had on India's trade, namely the creation of trading posts and forts along the Indian coast. The British East India Company, in particular, was a significant force in the development of India's economy as well as its commercial environment.

9. **Independence and Financial Reforms: An Emphasis on Self-Sufficiency**

The fight for independence from British colonial control in India resulted in a refocused attention on the importance of self-sufficiency and economic autonomy. India became an independent nation in 1947, and almost immediately began a process of economic modernization and advancement. The goal of this chapter is to achieve economic self-sufficiency, and to do so, we will study several policies, such as import substitution and governmental control over vital industries.

10. **The Modern Era and the Process of Globalization: The Rise of India as a Major Economic Player Worldwide**

India's meteoric rise to the status of economic powerhouse on the international stage may be traced back to the contemporary era. The Indian economy became more accessible to international commerce and investment when it underwent liberalization in the 1990s. This chapter goes at the role that India plays in the global economy, as well as its economic accomplishments and standing in international trade and diplomacy.

In the final chapter, we take some time to consider the ever-present relevance of business activity in India. In order to demonstrate how India's economic, cultural, and social growth have been influenced by trade, we will now weave together the various strands of history. This chapter emphasizes that India's trading heritage continues to play an important part in the nation's history, as well as its present and future, and that this legacy continues to contribute to India's growth and prosperity.

The purpose of this investigation into the development of trading in India is to offer readers with an in-depth comprehension of how trading practices have evolved over time in India, thereby influencing the nation's history, economy, culture, and interactions with the rest of the world. The development of trade in India over the course of history is not merely a chronicle of the past; rather, it is a demonstration of the ever-present significance of commerce in determining the character and trajectory of the nation.

1.1 Historical Overview

Trading is an age-old activity that has significantly influenced the development of human history, and this has never been more clear than it is in the history of the Indian subcontinent. A story of commerce, the sharing of culture, and the development of an economy that spans millennia is told in the context of an overview of the history of trading in India. The long and prosperous history of trade that India has had with other countries is evidence of the country's continuing importance in international commerce. During the course of this investigation, we will go through the historical landmarks that have marked India's trade tradition, beginning with the early days of barter systems and progressing all the way up to the present financial markets.

1. **An Overview of the Significance of India's Commercial Past**
   Before going into the historical context of trading in India, it is essential to emphasize the significance of this economic activity. This will set the stage for the subsequent discussion. Trading is not only the exchange of goods and services; rather, it is an essential force behind the expansion of the economy, the dissemination of culture, and the advancement of society. It played an essential role in the development of India's history, and one simply cannot stress the importance of this event in today's world.

2. **The early beginnings of the ancient system of bartering**
   The practice of bartering in earlier times can be traced back to the beginnings of commerce in India. People in a world without standardized currency would trade commodities directly with one another, making use of whatever extra resources they had available. This chapter goes into the early forms of commerce practiced in India and sheds light on how the practice of bartering paved the way for more advanced forms of commercial exchange.

3. **The Appearance of Coinage: A Revolutionary Development**
   The introduction of coinage represented a momentous turning point in the history of trade in India. This chapter examines the ways in which the establishment of standardized currency made commercial transactions more effective and made it possible to trade goods and services over wider distances. The circulation of coins was a major factor in the expansion of local and regional markets, as well as in the facilitation of economic growth.

4. **The Importance of India to the Silk Road**
   The Silk Road was an extensive network of trade routes that connected East and West and served as a conduit for the circulation of products, ideas, and cultural practices. The Indian subcontinent was connected to Central Asia, the Middle East, and other parts of the world through the southern branch of the Silk Road, which passed through India. India played a crucial role along this route. This chapter focuses on the contributions that India made to this historic trade route as well as its significance in the interchange of valuable commodities.

5. **The Spice Trade and India's Dominance in the Maritime World**
   Another historical commercial network that had a significant impact on India's economy and its ability to connect with the rest of the world was the Spice Trade. This chapter examines India's preeminent position in the maritime Spice Trade, focusing in especially on the Malabar Coast. The great demand for Indian spices such as black pepper, cardamom, and cinnamon throughout Europe and the Middle East led to the development of thriving trading networks in those regions.

6. **Medieval Communities Engaged in Commercial Exchange: the Cholas and the Pallavas**
   During the medieval period, various commercial societies in India, such as the Cholas and the Pallavas, played an important part in the development of India's marine trade. This chapter examines the marine endeavors of these great dynasties, their trade routes, and the influence that their commercial prowess had on the economics of India and the diplomacy of the surrounding region.

7. **Arab Merchants and the Emergence of India's Commercial Centers**
   Arab merchants created trading towns along the western coast of India, which significantly enhanced the commercial capacity of the nation. This chapter examines the impact that Arab merchants had on India's commercial hubs, as well as their participation in the Spice Trade and their contributions to the economy of India.

8. **The Mughal Empire was a thriving commercial center during its time.**
   The Mughal Empire, which lasted from 1526 until 1857, was a zenith in the history of trade in India. This chapter investigates the economic growth that occurred throughout the Mughal era, with a particular focus on the establishment of a monetary system, the creation of uniform currency, and the building of infrastructure to facilitate commerce. A look is also taken at India's booming textile industry, which results in the country's products being sold in many other countries around the world.

9. **The Influence of Other Powers During the Age of European Colonialism**
   The introduction of European colonial powers into India's trade environment, particularly the Portuguese, Dutch, French, and British, had a significant impact on the dynamics of the country's economy. The construction of trading posts, the struggle for control of India's commercial routes, and the influence of European colonialism on India's economy and society are all topics that are covered in this chapter.

10. **Rule by the British in the Colonies and Commercial Activity Under the British Raj**
    The British East India Company was responsible for the close incorporation of commercial activities within the structure of British colonial rule. This chapter goes into the economic exploitation of India's resources, the impact of British

colonial rule on trading practices, and the complicated legacy that the British Raj left behind.

11. **The Declaration of Independence of India and Its Economic Reforms**

    The fight for independence from British colonial control resulted in a refocused attention on self-reliance and economic autonomy. This chapter examines India's journey to independence as well as the country's subsequent efforts to restructure its economy.

    The goal of achieving economic self-sufficiency drove the creation of economic policies such as import substitution and state control over important industries.

12. **The Modern Era and the Liberalization of the Economy**

India has become one of the most significant economic powers on a global scale in the modern period. This chapter goes at the economic liberalization that took place in the 1990s in India, which paved the way for increased opportunities for international commerce and investment. This article investigates India's place in the international economy, as well as its economic achievements and standing in international trade and diplomacy.

In the final chapter, we take some time to consider the ever-present relevance of business activity in India. In order to demonstrate how India's economic, cultural, and social growth have been influenced by trade, we will now weave together the various strands of history. This chapter emphasizes that India's trading heritage continues to play an important part in the nation's history, as well as its present and future, and that this legacy continues to contribute to India's growth and prosperity.

An examination of the development of trade in India over time provides evidence of the country's continuing relevance in the international marketplace. It is not just a historical chronicle, but rather a narrative that is always evolving to reflect the changing economic, cultural, and social fabric of India. This summary highlights the ways in which India's trading heritage continues to play an important role in India's identity and its future.

1.2 Traditional Trade Practices

The history of trade in India is like a tapestry, with the threads of tradition, business, and cultural exchange intertwined throughout. Traditional business practices in India are illustrative of the nation's extensive commercial history. These activities encapsulate the spirit of cooperation and mutual benefit that has characterized India's economic environment for hundreds of years. In the course of this investigation, we dive into the conventional business methods that have played a significant role in the development of the nation's economy, culture, and society.

1. **An Introduction: The Importance of Using Conventional Business Procedures**

   It is essential that we acknowledge the significance of India's traditional business practices before we go into the particulars of those practices. Traditional business procedures are not only historical relics; rather, they are alive traditions that continue to have an impact on India's modern business landscape. They are a living embodiment of the values of reciprocity, community, and collaboration, and their continued existence is a tribute to the value that they have in the areas of economics, culture, and society.

2. **The Role of Bazaars and Haats in the Economy**

   Local bazaars and haats, often known as marketplaces, have played an essential role in the history of trade in India. Communities come together in these bustling marketplaces to trade items, talk to one another about their experiences, and celebrate the culture of their homeland. This chapter examines the historical significance of bazaars and haats, with a particular focus on their function in encouraging economic activity at the local level. It shines a light on the wide variety of goods—from spices and fabrics to handicrafts and agricultural produce—that make their way to these markets.

3. **The system of exchanging goods for services in the form of barter**

   In India, one of the earliest forms of commerce was the system of bartering goods and services. People used bartering, or the direct exchange of products and services, before the widespread use of currency. This chapter investigates the practice of bartering in both historical and modern settings. The goal is to provide light on how the barter system enabled societies to fulfill their requirements by exchanging surplus goods. Additionally investigated is the continued use of bartering methods in certain rural communities.

4. **Artisanal Production and Small-Scale Industries**

   Craftsmanship and home-based businesses have frequently been intertwined with India's long-established commercial customs and practices. This chapter goes into the history of skilled artisans and examines the role they played in the production of a wide variety of commodities, from elaborate jewelry to handwoven fabrics. It sheds light on the lasting significance of India's cottage industries and demonstrates how these businesses remain an integral component of the country's economic landscape.

5. **The Role Played by Community-Based Trade Guilds**

   Local trade guilds, also referred to as "shrenis" or "srenis," have been crucial in the organization of trade and the maintenance of fair business practices. This chapter dives into the historical significance of these guilds and their influence on numerous elements of trade, including the price of goods, the resolution of disputes, and quality control. The history of guilds and the relevance of guilds in today's society are both examined.

6. **The Silk Roads and Early Commercial Caravans**

   India has a long and illustrious tradition of taking part in various international commerce routes. This chapter discusses the Silk Routes, which were trade routes that linked India to other regions and made it easier for people to trade products and ideas with one another. It highlights the function of trade caravans, which braved difficult terrains in order to deliver valuable goods, as well as their contribution to international commerce.

7. **The Impact of Religious Centers and Public Markets**

   Throughout history, places of worship and public markets have served as hubs for commercial and cultural interaction. This chapter looks at the role that temples had in the development of commerce and how they acted as storage facilities for riches. Throughout history, fairs, particularly those that were affiliated with religious holidays, have been known to attract merchants and dealers from far and wide, which has contributed to the robustness of local economies.

8. **The Influence of Community- and Family-Owned Businesses**

   The commercial history of India is built on the foundation of family-owned and operated businesses. This chapter examines the significant role that family firms have had throughout history in maintaining traditional business practices. It explores the ways in which these firms have safeguarded the continuation of traditional craftsmanship, protected the authenticity of their products, and helped the communities in which they are located.

9. **The Impact of Conventional Financial Institutions and Methods**

Traditional banking systems of India, such as "hundi" and "chopda," have proven extremely helpful in easing the process of conducting business there. This chapter examines their relevance throughout history as well as their function in the trading community as providers of credit and other financial services. In addition to this, it analyzes how historic banking practices have influenced the development of contemporary financial institutions.

In the final chapter, we take some time to consider the persistent legacy that India's conventional modes of commerce have left behind. These customs have not been relegated to the dustbin of history but rather continue to thrive alongside the machinery of modern commerce. They exemplify the importance of community, sustainability, and the protection of cultural traditions. This chapter highlights the necessity of recognizing and conserving these traditional trade traditions as a vital component of India's economic, cultural, and social fabric. These customs have been around for centuries and have been passed down from generation to generation.

In India, traditional business practices constitute a dynamic and alive tradition that continues to have an impact on the nation's modern commerce scene. They serve as a reminder that the business world is about more than simply transactions; it is also about the relationships, communities, and cultural traditions that have helped define India's rich trading past.

1.3 Introduction of Formal Markets

The idea of formal markets is an essential component of the economic structure of a nation and functions as the central support system for all forms of organized commercial activity. The buying and selling of products and services takes place in a transparent, regulated, and orderly environment that is provided by formal markets. These markets also provide a level playing field for all of the market participants. The development of formal markets in India has been a significant factor in the country's overall economic expansion. This has had a profound impact on the nation's commercial landscape and helped elevate India's standing in the international economy. This investigation digs into the background of the establishment of formal marketplaces in India, charting their historical growth and analyzing their relevance in the modern era.

1. **The Importance of Formal Markets to Consider Introductory Remarks**
   It is imperative that prior to beginning our trip through the process of introducing formal markets in India, we must have a solid understanding of the significance of formal markets. These organized trading platforms are more than simply locations for the exchange of financial assets; rather, they are the epitome of structure, regulation, and transparency in the financial markets. Formal markets are extremely important to the formation of the economic landscape in India. These markets have an effect on a wide range of industries, including agriculture and banking, and they provide the basis for the expansion of the Indian economy.

2. **The Origins of Formal Markets in India, Historically Speaking**
   The establishment of organized markets in India has strong historical origins that go back to ancient times and may be traced all the way to modern times. This chapter investigates the historical roots of formal markets, with a particular focus on the role of "shrenis" or trade guilds, as well as the formation of organized marketplaces during India's medieval period. In addition to this, it illustrates the significance of formal marketplaces in aiding trade throughout history under the control of a variety of dynasties.

3. **The Impact That Colonialism and the British Raj Had On The World**
   The organization of trade and commerce in India saw considerable transformations throughout the time of British colonial rule. This chapter examines the effects that British colonialism had on formal markets, including the formation of the British East India Company as well as the construction of contemporary banking and commerce networks. In addition to this, it examines the ways in which British colonial power in India played a role in the formation of official marketplaces.

4. **The Functions of the State and Private Sectors in Economic Planning**
   Following the country's attainment of its independence in 1947, the Indian government was instrumental in formulating the country's economic policies

as well as the formal market structures. This chapter examines the impact that government planning had on the growth of a variety of economic institutions, as well as the role that planning had in that growth. In addition to this, it investigates the part that India's Planning Commission and its Five-Year Plans played in the formation of the country's formal market infrastructure.

5. **The Development of Stock Markets and Stock Exchanges**
A crucial component of the development of formal markets in India has been the creation of stock exchanges and their subsequent growth. This chapter explores the development of stock exchanges in India, beginning with the Bombay Stock Exchange (BSE) and progressing all the way up to the National Stock Exchange (NSE). This study looks at the role that India's various stock exchanges play in the expansion of India's financial sector by, among other things, providing a platform for the buying and selling of securities, influencing investment patterns, and contributing to India's overall economic development.

6. **Commodity Exchanges and Governmental Oversight**
The history of India's commodity markets is extensive, and the country's regulatory framework has developed significantly during the course of their existence. The evolution of commodities markets, such as the Multi commodities Exchange (MCX) and the National Commodity & Derivatives Exchange Limited (NCDEX), is investigated in this chapter. In addition to this, it discusses the function that regulatory agencies, such as the Forward Markets Commission (FMC), have in supervising the trade of commodities.

7. **Formal Markets in the Agricultural**
Agriculture is the backbone of India's economy, and the development of formal markets in the agricultural sector has been critical to both the increase in farmer income and the maintenance of adequate food supplies. Agricultural Produce Market Committees, sometimes known as APMCs, are discussed in this chapter, along with their function in the context of the regulation of agricultural trade. It also covers efforts to build a single national market for agricultural produce, such as the National Agriculture Market (e-NAM), which is one of the topics covered in this report.

8. **The Influence that Rapid Technological Advancement Has Had**
The formal markets in India have been completely disrupted as a result of the introduction of new technologies. This chapter explores the role that technology has played in the development of online trading platforms, the dematerialization of securities, and electronic trading in general. In addition to this, it investigates the impact that mobile applications and fintech companies have had on the availability and accessibility of formal markets.

9. **The Importance of Organized Markets to the Progress of the Economy**
Not only do formal markets serve as venues for business transactions, but they also serve as motors of economic growth. This chapter investigates the ways

in which formal markets contribute to the production of capital, the creation of jobs, and overall economic growth. It addresses the effects that they have on financial inclusion, investor protection, and the economic well-being of the nation as a whole.

10. **Obstacles and the Existing Regulatory Structure**

The establishment of legal markets in India has resulted in a variety of problems, such as increased market volatility and worries around regulatory oversight. This chapter discusses the difficulties and dangers that are connected to formal markets. Topics covered include issues concerning insider trading, market manipulation, and regulatory monitoring. In addition to this, it investigates the function that market regulators, such as the Securities and Exchange Board of India (SEBI), play in preserving the integrity of the market.

In the final chapter, we offer some thoughts on the current state of formal markets in India and their future prospects. The development of these organized trading platforms over the years has resulted in their incorporation into an essential part of India's overall economic framework. This chapter highlights their diverse significance in India's economic development, focusing on the impact that they have had on a variety of different industries as well as the growth trajectory of the nation.

In India, formal markets are not fixed entities but rather dynamic institutions that continue to develop along with the shifting economic landscape. They are the epitome of the ideals of transparency, regulation, and structured trade, and they provide a firm foundation for the growth and development of the nation's economic system. The purpose of this investigation into the formal markets that exist in India is to provide readers with a full grasp of the historical development of these markets as well as the relevance they hold in modern times.

1.4 Key Milestones in India's Trading History

Trading has a long and illustrious history in India, stretching back thousands of years and encompassing a wide variety of activities. India, which is one of the world's oldest civilizations, has been a prominent player in the global commerce network for a long time, contributing to the circulation of goods as well as ideas and cultures. Throughout the course of its history, India's commercial activity has been marked by a number of significant milestones that have influenced the country's economic, cultural, and political landscapes. During this in-depth investigation, we will investigate these landmarks, charting the development of India's trade from ancient times to the present day.

1. **Historic Passageways Through Which Goods Were Bartered and Bartered Goods**
   The Indus Valley Civilization flourished between the years 3300 and 1300 BCE:

The ancient Indus Valley Civilization, which was distinguished by well-planned cities, complex infrastructure, and a sophisticated trade network, may be traced back to the beginnings of India's trading history. This civilization can be found in the Indus Valley. The people who lived in the Indus Valley participated in trade with locations as far away as Mesopotamia and Egypt, sending goods such as textiles, spices, and precious metals in the other direction.

The Silk Road (about the second century BCE to the fourteenth century CE):

India was an essential node in the ancient commerce network known as the Silk Road, which linked East and West. Along the Silk Road, items such as silk, spices, textiles, precious stones, and even culture were freely traded with one another. This was made possible by the road's extensive network of trade routes. In the days of the ancient transcontinental commerce route, Indian traders were among the most active players.

The Spice Trade (about the first century CE):

In the ancient world, many spices, such as black pepper, cardamom, and cinnamon, were highly prized and sought after. The Roman Empire, the Middle East, and other regions all had commercial connections with India because of its prominent role as a producer and exporter of these spices. During this time period, India's economic growth was largely influenced by its participation in the spice trade.

2. **The Islamic Empires' Role in Medieval India and Their Impact on the Indian Subcontinent**

The Arab Trade (about in the seventh century CE):

The introduction of Islam and the subsequent growth of Islamic empires both paved the way for the development of new commercial routes connecting India and the Middle East. The Islamic world placed a high value on Indian textiles, spices, and luxury items, and Arab merchants created large trade networks with India to accommodate this demand.

The Delhi Sultanate, which existed roughly during the 13th and 16th centuries:

During the medieval period, the Delhi Sultanate, which reigned over a significant area of northern India, was an extremely influential force in the development of the commercial history of India. The trade policies of the Sultanate stimulated the interchange of goods with nearby regions, one of which was Central Asia.

The First Portuguese Settlers Arrive (in the late 15th century):

The arrival of Portuguese explorer Vasco da Gama in Calicut in 1498 marked the beginning of European engagement in the commercial activities of India. The Portuguese monopoly on the spice trade had a significant influence on the history of trade in India because of the tremendous impact it had on the spice trade. In addition to this, they were instrumental in the introduction of Indian items to the market in Europe.

3. **The Mughals and the European Colonial Powers in the Third Age of Empires**

The Mughal Empire lasted roughly from the 16th to the 18th century.

The Mughal Empire, which was one of the most powerful empires in Indian history, contributed significantly to the legacy of trade and commerce. It established a coordinated framework that facilitated commerce by preserving order and promoting security along important trade corridors. The Mughals were also responsible for standardizing monetary practices, which made it easier for people to do business.

Powers in Europe That Had Colonial Empires:

From the 16th to the 19th century, European colonial powers engaged in a power struggle for control over India's huge resources. Trading businesses and colonial outposts were formed in various regions of India by the British, Dutch, French, and Portuguese empires. These colonial powers took advantage of India's richness, which resulted in the deindustrialization of certain areas of the country.

The British East India Company (active roughly during the 17th and 19th centuries):

During the time period when India was under colonial rule, the British East India Company was an extremely influential force in the development of India's commercial history. It created a monopoly on important trading routes and resources, like as cotton, opium, and tea, among other things. The expansion of the British Empire's sphere of influence in India over time eventually resulted in the colonization of the whole subcontinent.

The Opium Trade (about throughout the 18th and 19th centuries):

During the time of British colonial rule in India, the opium trade was an important part of the country's trading history. The opium that was produced in India was traded with China, which led to disastrous results for both countries. The Opium Wars in China were partially caused by the opium trade, which is an example of the global impact of the opium industry.

4. **The Struggle for Independence and the Economic Revolution**

Movement of Swadeshi (around the beginning of the 20th century):

The Swadeshi Movement was an important one in India's trading history because it marked a turning point in the fight for independence from British colonial control. This made it a crucial milestone in India's overall history. Indians advocated for the use of locally manufactured commodities and rejected British imports, which sparked a sense of economic independence for the Indian people.

The Consequences of World War II, Which Lasted From 1939 to 1945:

The impact that World War II had on India's trading history was significant and far-reaching. The conflict caused disruptions in international trade, which in turn led to shortages of necessary products. Because of India's contribution to the war effort, considerable adjustments were made to the country's economic policies, with an increased focus on self-sufficiency.

Independence and Economic Planning (from 1947 to the 1960s):

The year 1947 marked the beginning of a new era in the history of India's commercial activity. The nation adopted a planned economic approach, with the Five-Year Plans aiming to strengthen domestic sectors and reduce dependency on imports. The country also adopted a planned economic approach. The pursuit of economic self-sufficiency served as the guiding principle for the formulation of trade policy.

5. **The Economies of Globalization and Liberalization in Contemporary India**

The Liberalization of the Economy (1991):

The year 1991 marked a watershed moment in India's economic history because it was the year that economic liberalization policies were put into effect. Trade was liberalized, tariffs were lowered, and the Indian economy was opened up to foreign investment as a result of these changes, which were spearheaded by Prime Minister Narasimha Rao and Finance Minister Manmohan Singh.

India's Information Technology Boom (in the late 20th century):

In the latter half of the 20th century, India established itself as a leading center for information technology (IT) and software services worldwide. This industry made a considerable contribution to India's total export revenues and was an essential cog in the economic expansion of the country.

The Green Revolution (roughly spanning the decades 1960–1970):

Because of the huge rise in agricultural output that it brought about, the Green Revolution was an important event in the history of India's commercial sector. India has become a self-sufficient food producer and even a net exporter of food grains as a result of the adoption of innovative farming practices and the introduction of crop varieties with increased potential yields.

The 21st Century's Bilateral Trade Agreements (BTAs):

In the 21st century, India has significantly increased its participation in bilateral trade agreements with a wide variety of countries and areas. Because of these accords, trade has been made easier by the elimination of trade restrictions, the encouragement of exports, and the improvement of economic cooperation.

6. **Obstacles and Prospects in the History of India's Commercial Activities**

The Development of Infrastructure:

The growth of India's infrastructure is intimately connected to its long and prosperous history of trade. It is essential to make investments in transportation, ports, and logistics in order to guarantee a continuous and uninterrupted flow of goods both locally and globally.

Trade Deficits and Balance of Trade:

Recent years have shown trade deficits for India, which indicates that the country has been importing more goods than it has been exporting. The nation's economic officials face a huge issue in the form of a significant problem when it comes to managing trade imbalances.

Integration of International Supply Chains:

The amount of time that India spends contributing to global supply chains has gone up, particularly in the manufacturing and technology industries. This integration has opened up potential for expansion but has also brought obstacles in terms of regulatory compliance and competitiveness.

Considerations Regarding International Politics:

The history of trade in India has been shaped by geopolitics, particularly the country's connections with its immediate neighbors and the world's most powerful nations. Tensions in geopolitical affairs have the potential to impact trade relations and business strategies.

Concerns Regarding the Environment and Sustainability:

As a result of the country's continuing economic expansion, India is coming under an increasing amount of pressure to address issues of sustainability and environmental protection that are connected to commercial and industrial endeavors.

Ancient trade, medieval empires, colonial exploitation, independence wars, and modern economic upheavals are woven together in India's commerce history to create a complex tapestry. The passage of time in this nation has witnessed the establishment of trade routes, the extraction of resources, the growth of an economy that is both vigorous and diverse, and the rise and fall of numerous empires. India has undergone consistent development and adaptation throughout its history, from the ancient Silk Road to the current information technology boom, in order to keep pace with the shifting dynamics of the global economy.

India will continue to be a key player in international trade and commerce; as a result, it will continue to face a variety of opportunities and problems. It takes careful planning, strategic investments, and an eye toward sustainability in order to strike a balance between the demands of a quickly changing global landscape and the organization's rich past. The history of India's trade is evidence of the country's resiliency and adaptability, and the country's future holds the potential of sustained economic expansion and increased influence in international markets.

Chapter 2

The Role of Trading in Economic Growth

Since the dawn of time, international commerce has been an essential engine for economic expansion. It has enabled the free flow of commodities, services, and ideas across geographical areas and national borders. Throughout the course of human history, commerce has been an essential factor in the growth of economies, the production of new jobs, the elevation of living standards, and the promotion of new ideas. This all-encompassing investigation digs into the complex relationship that exists between commerce and economic expansion. It examines the ways in which trade processes, laws, and globalization have influenced the development of economies and cultures all over the world.

1. **The Monetary and Financial Underpinnings of Commerce**
   The Meaning of Trade and Its Fundamentals
   Trade refers to the buying and selling of commodities and services between different parties, including individuals, businesses, and nations. It is possible for it to take many different forms, such as bartering, monetary transactions, and even e-commerce. The concept of trade is essential to the study of economics and is the cornerstone of market-based economies.
   Advantages of Comparative Competition and Specialization:
   David Ricardo is credited as being the one who first proposed the idea of comparative advantage as a foundation for the study of international trade. According to this thesis, there is a basis for commerce that is beneficial to both parties involved even if one nation is less efficient at manufacturing all things compared to another one. Productivity gains and a general expansion of the economy might result from a nation's increasing emphasis on the production of those goods and services in which it holds a comparative advantage over other nations.
   Profits Obtained via Trade:
   Trade enables the effective distribution of resources, which in turn encourages

the expansion of economic activity. Countries that participate in trade have the potential to benefit by gaining access to a greater variety of goods, paying less for those goods, and having more possibilities to sell their own goods on international markets.

2. **Historical Perspectives on the Relationship Between Trade and Economic Growth**

Ancient Transportation Networks:

Trade routes connected ancient civilizations such as Mesopotamia, the Roman Empire, and the Indus Valley, making it possible for products to be traded and for culture to spread from one region to another. Silk, spices, and ideas were just some of the things that flowed freely between different civilizations thanks to the Silk Road, which connected the East and the West.

Mercantilism: the period between the 16th and 18th centuries:

European nations embraced mercantilist policies throughout the Age of Exploration and colonial expansion. These policies had the goal of amassing wealth through trade surpluses and the purchase of colonies. These policies led to exploitative activities as well as disputes, but they did encourage economic growth in several European countries, which was a positive outcome.

The Industrial Revolution, which occurred between the 18th and 19th centuries:

Mechanization and mass production were two aspects of economic life that were fundamentally altered as a result of the Industrial Revolution. The movement of raw materials and finished commodities helped to facilitate economic growth, which was facilitated in large part by trade, which played a vital role in aiding the rise of industrialization.

3. **Contemporary Economic Hypotheses Concerning Growth and Trade**

Model of Hecksher and Ohlin:

The Hecksher-Ohlin model elaborates on the idea of comparative advantage by highlighting the fact that nations export commodities that make use of abundant elements of production (such as labor and capital), while at the same time they import goods that make use of scarce factors. This model sheds light on how international commerce can contribute to the effective utilization of resources and increased economic growth.

The Emerging Concept of Trade:

Paul Krugman is often credited as being the driving force behind the New Trade Theory, which places an emphasis on the role that economies of scale and product differentiation play in international trade. This demonstrates how better production efficiency and access to a wider variety of goods can both contribute to economic expansion through the medium of trade.

The theory of endogenous growth:

The relationship between innovation, technological advancement, and international trade is investigated by endogenous growth theory, which has been promoted by economists such as Paul Romer. It proposes that more commerce can stimulate economic growth by promoting the dissemination of information, which in turn leads to advances in technology and higher levels of productivity.

4. **Economic Expansion and the Role of Trade Policies**

Tariffs and other Obstacles to Trade:

The installation of tariffs and other trade barriers can be detrimental to economic growth since it restricts access to international markets, drives up the price of imported goods, and may even cause trade wars to break out. Eliminating or lessening the impact of such obstacles on economic growth might be beneficial.

Agreements Regarding Free Trade:

Free trade agreements (also known as FTAs) are negotiated between countries or regions in an effort to lower existing trade barriers and increase market access. These agreements have the potential to increase market access and enhance international cooperation, both of which are beneficial to economic growth.

Exportation Marketing:

When governments want to encourage economic growth, they will frequently pursue measures that promote exports. To assist local enterprises in expanding their export activity, these techniques may include monetary incentives, trade missions, and marketing initiatives.

Substitution of Import Goods:

The term "import substitution industrialization," or "ISI," refers to a method whereby a nation works to lessen its reliance on imported commodities by cultivating its own domestic manufacturing sector. Although ISI may be beneficial in the short run, there is a possibility that it will hinder economic growth over the longer term due to inefficiencies and a lack of competition.

5. **The Process of Globalization and Its Effects**

Globalization and the Expansion of the Economy:

The current period has been witness to the quickening pace of globalization, which may be defined as the unrestricted movement of capital, goods, information, and labor across international borders. Globalization has had a positive impact on economic growth by increasing the number of available markets and boosting levels of competition. However, it has also brought about problems such as increased inequality, cultural assimilation, and environmental concerns.

MNCs, sometimes known as multinational corporations:

Because of their reach across borders, multinational firms have been an essential driving force behind globalization. They stimulate economic expansion by generating new employment opportunities, funding improvements in physical infrastructure, and acting as a conduit for the international exchange of technological know-how and specialized expertise.

Recent Advances in Technology:

The Information Age has been a significant contributor to the process of globalization as well as economic expansion. The use of digital technology, such as the internet, has fundamentally altered the way in which businesses conduct their daily operations, interact with their clientele, and take part in international commerce.

6. **Perspectives from Various Regions on Commerce and Economic Development**

The Miracle of East Asia:

During the second part of the 20th century, a number of East Asian countries, such as South Korea, Taiwan, and Singapore, enjoyed a period of rapid economic expansion. This phenomenon is commonly referred to as the "East Asian Miracle." These nations placed a strong emphasis on education, technology, and innovation while also utilizing exports and international trade as engines of economic expansion.

The European Union (EU) includes:

The European Union serves as a paradigmatic illustration of economic integration across multiple regions. While the single market and customs union have helped member states increase their trade and economic output, they have also created obstacles for the member states in the areas of sovereignty and coordination.

Both NAFTA and the USMCA:

Both the North American Free Trade Agreement (NAFTA) and its successor, the United States-Mexico-Canada Agreement (USMCA), have played an essential role in fostering increased economic activity and commerce across the North American continent. They place a strong emphasis on market access as well as the liberalization of commerce within the region.

7. **Trade and Inclusive Growth**

Unequal Distribution of Income:

Trade has the potential to increase income inequality, despite the fact that it can be a driver of economic progress. There is a possibility that the benefits of commerce do not flow evenly throughout the population, with some parts of the population potentially benefiting more than others.

Goals for Sustainable Development (also known as the SDGs):

Trade is recognized as an important component in the achievement of inclusive, sustainable, and equitable economic growth as one of the Sustainable Development Goals outlined by the United Nations. The alleviation of poverty, maintenance of a healthy environment, and parity between the sexes are all ideals that are connected with trade.

Trade that is Fair and Trade that is Ethical:

Initiatives promoting fair trade have the overarching goal of ensuring that workers in developing nations are compensated fairly and can do their jobs in an ethical manner. Consumers that are interested in purchasing goods that meet certain social and environmental criteria have a strong interest in ethical trading practices.

8. **Obstacles to Overcome and Contentious Debate**
Deficits and Surpluses in International Trade
Both sustained trade deficits and sustained trade surpluses have the potential to be sources of economic instability. Countries that run significant trade deficits are more likely to rack up debt, whereas countries that run trade surpluses may be subject to political pressures to revalue their currencies.

Trade Conflicts:
Both the United States and China are currently engaged in a trade war, which has the potential to disrupt global trade and slow economic growth.

The imposition of tariffs, other limitations on imports, and retaliatory measures can result in a contraction of economic activity as well as uncertainty in the market.

Concerns Regarding the Environment:
The expansion of international trade has given rise to a number of environmental issues, such as the emission of carbon dioxide (CO_2) from transportation and the cutting down of trees due to the production of specific items. The adoption of environmentally responsible business practices and laws is absolutely necessary in order to solve these challenges.

Aspects of International Politics:
Trade routes and the consistency of international trade are both susceptible to disruption when geopolitical tensions, such as territorial conflicts and security concerns, are present. Disruptions in important trading regions are possible when there is political instability in those regions.

9. **The Prospects for Commercial Activity and Economic Expansion**

The Digital Economy:
The global economy is on the verge of being revolutionized by the rise of digital trade, which will be propelled by e-commerce and the trading of digital services. This type of commerce extends beyond the conventional borders of nations and opens up new opportunities for economic expansion.

Resilience of the Supply Chain:
The epidemic caused by COVID-19 brought to light vulnerabilities in global supply chains. The pursuit of supply chain resilience, also known as "reshoring" or "nearshoring," has become a goal for both nations and enterprises. These terms are often used interchangeably.

New or Developing Markets:

Opportunities for both commercial expansion and general monetary expansion can be found in emerging economies such as those found in Africa and Southeast Asia. They are distinguished by expanding consumer markets, higher rates of urbanization, and opportunities for business investment.

Trade is an essential component that propels economic expansion, which in turn encourages wealth, innovation, and connection on a global scale. Trade has been an essential factor in the development of economies all over the world, whether one looks at it through the lens of more traditional ideas like comparative advantage or more modern perspectives on the part that technology and innovation play.

While trade has the capacity to promote inclusive growth and shared prosperity, it also raises difficulties linked to inequality, environmental sustainability, and geopolitical conflicts. While trade has the potential to promote inclusive growth and shared prosperity, it also has the potential to create these challenges.

Understanding the complex nature of the relationship that exists between economic growth and commerce is vital in light of the ongoing evolution of the global economy. The complexity of international commerce must be navigated by policymakers, entrepreneurs, and societies in order to reap the benefits of trade while also tackling the issues it presents. By doing so, they can assist ensure that trade continues to serve as a driver of economic progress that is to the advantage of individuals, nations, and the global community as a whole.

2.1 The Economic Significance of Trading

Trading is an essential component of the global economy since it facilitates the flow of products, services, and resources across countries. This makes it one of the most important aspects of the economy. Its influence extends far beyond mere transactions, having an effect not just on employment but also on investment, innovation, and the expansion of the economy as a whole. This all-encompassing investigation looks deeply into the multidimensional economic significance of trading, investigating, among other things, the contributions it has made to the production of wealth, the expansion of markets, and international collaboration.

1. **Employment and the Changing Nature of the Labor Market**
   Creating New Jobs:
   Trading activities, in both their direct and indirect forms, contribute greatly to the development of new jobs. Trade-related activities create job opportunities and help drive economic growth. These activities support a varied range of professions, from exporters and manufacturers to retailers and suppliers of logistics services.

   The development of specific competencies and areas of expertise:
   The expansion of international trade fosters specialization and enables nations to concentrate their production efforts on those items and services in which they hold a competitive advantage over other nations. This specialization encourages

the development of specialized skills and expertise, which ultimately results in an increase in both productivity and competitiveness in the global economy.

Mobility of labor and the international workforce:

The interconnection of global markets, which is made possible by trade, has led to an increase in labor mobility, which enables individuals to look for employment possibilities in a variety of nations. The increased mobility of workers around the world has improved labor markets and made it easier to share information and expertise across national boundaries.

2. **The Generation of Wealth and the Acceleration of Economic Growth**
   Development of New Markets:

   Trading creates new markets for goods and services, enabling companies to sell to a more diverse group of customers both within and outside of their own country's borders. Having access to worldwide markets helps to boost demand, which in turn increases output and contributes to economic expansion.

   Productivity that is Greater:

   As a result of increased rivalry brought about by more trade, businesses are able to increase their level of efficiency and productivity as they attempt to create high-quality items at lower prices. This rivalry serves as an incentive for innovation, the expansion of technological capabilities, and the adoption of best practices, all of which ultimately contribute to economic growth.

   FDI stands for "foreign direct investment"

   Trade liberalization and market openness are two factors that attract foreign direct investment (FDI). FDI is beneficial to economic growth because it provides capital, facilitates the transfer of technology, and creates employment possibilities. The growth of infrastructure and industry in host nations is aided by foreign direct investment (FDI) inflows, which are frequently driven by advantageous trade policies.

3. **Innovation as well as progress made in technological areas**
   Transferring of Knowledge:

   The free flow of information between nations, including new concepts, methodologies, and technologies, is made possible by international trade. This information transfer helps to stimulate innovation and technical improvement, and it enables firms to embrace and adapt cutting-edge technology from around the world. As a result, these enterprises become more competitive and contribute to economic growth.

   Investigation and Experimentation:

   When companies compete on a global scale, they must make significant investments in research and development (R&D) to maintain their competitive edge. Research and development operations that focus on enhancing existing products, lowering production costs, and developing new technologies all contribute to the development of innovative products and services, which in turn helps the economy advance and remain competitive.

Effects that Reverberate:

The benefits of innovation that is stimulated by trade can have ripple effects that are felt not just by individual companies but also by entire industries and economies. It is possible for the spread of technology and knowledge across international borders to result in the establishment of new economic sectors, the improvement of existing industries, and an increase in the economic output of the entire economy.

4. **Trade Deficits and the Value of the Foreign Currency**

   Trade Effort and Its Balance:

   A crucial economic statistic that is affected by trading activity is the balance of trade, which is defined as the difference between a country's exports and imports. A continuous trade deficit may put strain on an economy, while a positive trade balance, which indicates stronger exports than imports, can help to economic growth. A negative trade balance, on the other hand, indicates that imports were higher than exports.

   Reserves de Change de Valeur Monétaire:

   Trade results in earnings denominated in a foreign currency, which provide a contribution to a nation's foreign exchange reserves. A nation's ability to manage its currency rates and maintain stability in international trade and financial transactions is dependent on its holding sufficient amounts of foreign exchange reserves. These reserves serve as a buffer against the effects of external shocks.

   Evaluation of the Currency:

   Trading activities have an effect on the valuation of a currency, with a robust export industry often leading to an increase in the value of the local currency. A more favorable currency valuation can be advantageous for consumers since it can make imported items more affordably priced, but a weaker currency can increase export competitiveness and help economic growth.

5. **Integration of Regional Economies and Cooperation on the Global Stage**

   The formation of economic blocs and free trade agreements:

   Trade and investment are encouraged among participating nations as a result of regional economic integration, which is supported through trade agreements and economic blocs. Regional cooperation is facilitated by organizations such as the European Union, the Association of Southeast Asian Nations (ASEAN), and the African Continental Free Trade Area (AfCFTA), all of which work to lower trade barriers and build larger, more integrated markets.

   Relations and Collaboration in the Diplomatic Arena:

   The development of diplomatic ties and international cooperation is facilitated by commercial exchange, which in turn serves as a forum for communication and coordination between nations. Trade agreements frequently contribute to political stability, cultural interchange, and the development of global peace and understanding in addition to their economic benefits.

Resolution and Avoidance of Future Conflicts:

Trading partnerships can act as a buffer against disputes because they establish interdependencies that prevent acts that could be construed as confrontational. Interdependencies are created when mutually beneficial economic links are created. Trading can help contribute to the prevention of conflicts and the resolution of international disputes by fostering cooperative behavior and the pursuit of mutual interests.

6. **Repercussions on Society and the Environment**

Growth in Social Conditions:

Trading's economic significance extends to social development in the sense that an increase in economic activity and employment possibilities contribute to a reduction in poverty, an improvement in living standards, and expanded access to educational opportunities and medical care. Sustainable business practices can help to create inclusive growth, which is to the benefit of vulnerable demographic groups and marginalized communities.

Sustainability in Relation to the Environment:

Although increased trade helps fuel economic expansion, it also has repercussions for the natural world. Sustainable business practices, such as eco-friendly production techniques, the utilization of renewable energy sources, and responsible resource management, are absolutely necessary for minimizing the negative effects that commercial operations have on the surrounding environment and ensuring the planet's continued well-being in the long run.

CSR stands for "corporate social responsibility"

As a part of their day-to-day operations, a lot of companies do things that fall under the category of "corporate social responsibility." CSR programs that focus on community development, environmental protection, and ethical business practices contribute to sustainable and responsible trading, which promotes beneficial social and environmental results. CSR programs are also known as corporate social responsibility programs.

7. **Obstacles to Overcome and Potential Benefits**

Protectionism and Economic Conflicts:

The global trading system is faced with considerable obstacles when protectionist policies, trade disputes, and trade wars are in play. Because of these activities, supply chains are disrupted, trade prices are increased, and economic growth is stifled, all of which create uncertainty for businesses as well as for consumers.

Disruptions Caused by New Technologies:

Rapid technology breakthroughs, including as automation and digitalization, are transforming the face of global trade. These changes are likely to have a significant impact. These technological disruptions, while creating new opportunities for efficiency and creativity, also present obstacles in the form of job displacement and the requirement for retraining and further education of the labor force.

Vulnerabilities within the Global Supply Chain:

As a result of disruptions in manufacturing, logistics, and trade flows, the COVID-19 pandemic brought to light the vulnerability of global supply systems. Businesses and regulators are investigating solutions to manage risks and promote supply chain resilience in an effort to meet the growing demand for robust and diversified supply networks.

The activity of trading goods and services is essential to the functioning of the global economy since it is the primary driver of economic expansion, employment, innovation, and international cooperation. Its significance to the economy extends to a wide variety of spheres, including the labor markets, the generation of wealth, the advancement of technology, and the growth of society. Trading involves a number of obstacles, including protectionism, technology disruptions, and supply chain weaknesses; nevertheless, it also presents a number of opportunities for economic growth and international cooperation. To fully realize the economic potential of trade while simultaneously ensuring that its benefits are distributed fairly among all nations and communities, it is vital to find ways to adapt to the difficulties that lie ahead and to develop trading practices that are both sustainable and inclusive.

2.2 Trading's Contribution to GDP

Trade, which includes both exports and imports, is an essential component of the economic picture that can be painted of a nation as a whole. The contribution that commerce makes to a nation's Gross Domestic Product (GDP) is among the most important ways in which it stimulates economic activity. The gross domestic product (GDP) of a country is a crucial indicator of the state of its economy because it measures the nation's overall economic output. During the course of this conversation, we are going to investigate the myriad of ways in which economic activities like trading can have an impact on a nation's GDP, as well as evaluate the significance of economic activity like trading in fostering growth and development.

1. **Having an Understanding of GDP**

   It is necessary to have a solid understanding of what GDP stands for before digging into the role that trading plays in the overall economy. The gross domestic product (GDP) of a nation is the sum total of the value of all the products and services that are produced inside its boundaries over a particular period of time, which is commonly measured on an annual or quarterly basis. It is determined through the utilization of the following basic methodologies: production, spending, and revenue.

   According to the production method, GDP is calculated by adding up the value of all of the goods and services that are created inside the nation.

   The gross domestic product (GDP) is calculated using the expenditure method by adding up all of the money spent on goods and services. This method takes into account consumption, investment, government expenditures, and net exports.

The gross domestic product (GDP) is calculated using the income technique by adding up all of the income that the various components of production make, such as their wages, rents, interest, and profits.

2. **The Contribution of Business to Gross Domestic Product**

Exports and the Output of the Economy:

The value of a nation's gross domestic product (GDP) is directly influenced by the commodities and services that it sells to consumers in other countries. A nation's Gross Domestic Product (GDP) will benefit from having a trade surplus if it is able to produce more revenue from exports than it does from imports. The exporting industries, which can include everything from manufacturing to agriculture, are extremely important to the overall growth and output of the economy.

Consumption at home compared to that of imported goods

Imports, which are defined as products and services purchased from a foreign country, are another factor that influences GDP. Imports may have a negative impact on a nation's gross domestic product (GDP) when calculated using the expenditure method; but, they do contribute to domestic consumption, which is a key component of GDP. The availability of imported goods offers customers access to a greater selection of products and may result in cost reductions.

Economic Stability:

The difference between a country's total exports and total imports is known as the trade balance. A trade surplus, which occurs when exports are higher than imports, contributes to the GDP, but a trade deficit, which occurs when imports are higher than exports, can reduce GDP. It is important for governments and economists to keep a careful eye on the impact that the trade balance has on GDP since it shows the state of a nation's commercial connections.

Investing and the Circulation of Capital:

A nation's GDP can also be affected by trade in another way: through foreign direct investment (FDI). Increased output, the creation of new jobs, and the expansion of infrastructure are typical outcomes for a nation that is successful in luring foreign direct investment from multinational corporations. Foreign direct investment (FDI) can have a major impact on a country's GDP by increasing that country's overall productive capacity.

Effects on the Supply Chain:

The production and distribution of goods have been significantly altered as a result of the development of global supply chains, which has been pushed by international trade. Each stage of a product's journey through the supply chain is an opportunity to add value and make a contribution to GDP. Trading has an effect on the GDP at a number of different points throughout the supply chain, beginning with the extraction of raw materials and continuing through manufacture, transportation, and retail.

3. **The Role of Commerce in Gross Domestic Product:**

Use of resources (C):

The amount of money spent by consumers is a significant contributor to GDP, and international trade has a direct impact on the range of consumer goods that are both available and affordable to consumers. Access to items created in other countries broadens the range of options available to consumers and drives up total consumption levels.

The word "Investment" (I):

The term "investment expenditure" refers to the money that a company spends on purchasing capital goods like machinery and equipment. Imports of capital goods and foreign direct investment (FDI), both of which can boost investment and overall GDP, are two ways that trade can have an effect on this category.

Spending by the Government (G):

Spending by governments is another factor that goes into calculating GDP. Trade can have an effect on this factor through the purchasing of goods and services by governments, particularly imports that are tied to defense and infrastructure.

Exports After Imports (X-M):

Under the expenditure method, the Gross Domestic Product (GDP) is directly impacted by net exports, which can be defined as the difference between total exports (X) and total imports (M). A positive result for net exports (exports more than imports) contributes to GDP, whereas a negative value for net exports (imports greater than exports) detracts from it.

4. **Opportunities and Obstacles Relating to International Trade:**

The principle of protectionism:

Trade policies, such as tariffs and other forms of trade restriction, have the potential to impede

economic growth and trade flows. There is a risk of retaliation and trade wars if protectionist measures are implemented, which would create uncertainty for consumers and businesses.

The Disruption Caused by Technology

Trade and the economic impact it has are undergoing fundamental transformations as a result of developments in technology such as e-commerce and automation. Although new technologies can improve productivity and the rate of innovation, they also have the potential to disrupt job markets and trade balances.

Vulnerabilities within the Global Supply Chain:

The epidemic caused by COVID-19 brought to light vulnerabilities in global supply chains. It is necessary to ensure the resilience and flexibility of supply chains in order to prevent disruptions in trade and to keep economic growth at its current level.

Trade that is Both Sustainable and Inclusive:

Both policymakers and businesses are coming to realize the need of promoting trade that is both sustainable and inclusive. It's possible that business practices that take into account social and environmental considerations could result in more fair economic growth and better benefits for society.

The contribution that trading has made to GDP cannot be refuted, and this fact exemplifies the interconnection of the economies of the world. The level of economic output, as well as consumption and investment patterns, as well as the balance of trade, are all impacted by exports and imports. Case studies of countries like Germany, China, and the United States provide light on the relevance of commerce in generating GDP growth. These countries are all examples of free trade economies. The benefit that trade has on GDP, however, is not without its drawbacks, such as protectionism, technology upheavals, and supply chain weaknesses.

In the 21st century, the role that commerce plays in GDP is shifting in response to developments in technology, changes in global supply networks, and an increased emphasis on environmentally responsible business practices. To successfully navigate the global economic environment and make the most of the opportunities and difficulties that are given by international trade, it is vital for nations and enterprises to have a solid understanding of the complexities involved in the contribution that trading has made to GDP.

2.3 Job Creation and Trading

The relationship between job creation and trading is a symbiotic one that is also dynamic. This relationship reflects the delicate interplay that exists between economic activities within a nation and its interactions with the global economy. Trading activities, which include both domestic and international commerce, play an essential part in the creation of employment opportunities. These activities affect not just the total number of jobs within an economy but also the quality of those positions. In the following discussion, we will investigate how activities related to trading can help to create new jobs, as well as the numerous ways in which this relationship might have an effect on the labor markets, industries, and general economic development.

1. **Employment That Is Directly Linked To The Trade Industry:**
   Commerce at the Retail and Wholesale Levels:
   The wholesale and retail sectors of commerce are the principal recipients of benefits from trading activity. In order to satisfy the needs of their customers, retail establishments rely on a sizable labor force that consists of sales associates, cashiers, and shop managers.
   Distribution, inventory management, and logistics are only few of the operations

that are involved in wholesale commerce, which results in the creation of job possibilities in supply chain management and transportation.

The following industries are considered to be export-oriented:

Manufacturing and production industries have strong ties to global commerce and economic exchange. The demand for manufactured items, such as vehicles, electronics, and machinery, is a driving force behind the creation of new jobs within these industries. Manufacturing employment are created in export-oriented industries such as textiles, electronics, and automobiles. These positions not only satisfy home need but also satisfy demand from around the world.

Transport and Logistical Considerations:

Transportation and logistics services are extremely important to the success of commercial trade. There is a diverse array of work available in this industry, ranging from truck drivers and people who handle freight to people who work in customs and supply chain analysis. The transportation of commodities, both within the country and between countries, is an essential component in the process of job development within various industries.

2. **Job Creation Through Indirect Means in Support Industries:**

   The Worlds of Finance and Banking:

   In order to ease transactions, coordinate foreign payments, and provide trade finance, commercial activities frequently necessitate the services of financial intermediaries and banking institutions. There are a variety of positions available for employment in the financial sector, such as those in banks, as financial analysts, and as trade finance experts.

   Services in the Fields of Law and Regulation:

   The legal and regulatory systems that govern international trade can be somewhat complicated. It is the responsibility of lawyers, compliance officers, and government officials working in trade-related fields to guarantee that trading activities correspond to legal and regulatory norms. As a result, job creation can be attributed to the legal and compliance professions.

   Information and Communication Technology:

   Technology plays a crucial part in the facilitation of trade in this age of digitalization. Jobs in information technology and digital infrastructure, such as software developers, cybersecurity experts, and data analysts, are very necessary in order to guarantee the uninterrupted operation of trading activities.

3. **Micro, small, and medium-sized businesses (also known as SMEs):**

   Within the ecosystem of commerce, small and medium-sized businesses are frequently the primary drivers of job creation. Small and medium-sized businesses (SMEs) commonly participate in domestic as well as international trade, providing goods and services that target specialized markets or particular industries. These companies are well-known for their nimbleness and adaptability in the face of fluctuating market conditions; in addition, the growth of these enterprises instantly translates into job possibilities.

4. **The Influence on the Labor Markets:**

Multiple Possibilities for Gaining Employment:

Trading activities offer a diverse range of career options, which are suitable for people with a variety of educational backgrounds, skill sets, and levels of professional experience. Trade provides a wide variety of work opportunities suitable for job seekers with varying levels of experience and expertise, ranging from entry-level positions in retail to highly specialized professions in logistics.

Improvement of Abilities and Instruction:

Investing in education and training is encouraged because of the demand for a knowledgeable labor force to underpin commercial activity. This promotes the growth of workers' skills as well as learning that continues throughout life, so increasing their employability. Certifications in areas such as international business, supply chain management, and logistics are sometimes included in training programs.

Influence on the Jobless Rate:

Successful commercial activities can contribute to a decrease in the unemployment rate by taking up a share of the available labor. The expansion of businesses to fulfill rising demands typically results in the hiring of additional workers, which contributes to a decrease in the unemployment rate within a region or country.

5. **Obstacles and Things to Take Into Account:**

The Disruption Caused by Technology

The employment environment in sectors associated to commerce is being disrupted by technological developments in areas such as automation, robots, and artificial intelligence. Even though automation can improve efficiency and productivity, it also has the potential to eliminate jobs in particular industries, making it necessary for workers to adjust their skills and undergo retraining.

Respect for Workers' Rights and Ethical Work Practices:

It is essential to take measures to ensure that jobs created through commercial activity adhere to all applicable labor rights and fair employment practices. Trade is occasionally linked to the exploitation of labor and to working conditions that are deplorable, which is why there needs to be oversight and rules in place to protect workers' rights.

Responsibility to the Community and Environmental Stewardship:

To a greater extent, the ideals of sustainability and social responsibility must be incorporated into trading activities. Businesses that emphasize environmentally friendly products, ethical labor standards, and community engagement are contributing to a greener economy by prioritizing sustainable trade practices.

The formation of new jobs and the expansion of existing ones are intricately intertwined, producing a mutually beneficial connection that is essential to the expansion and growth of the economy. Trading operations create employment opportunities not only in areas directly related to trading, but also in a variety of industries that support trading, such as banking, legal services, and technology. This varied terrain of employment presents chances for a wide variety of people, from workers with no specific training to experts with the highest level of expertise.

Nevertheless, this partnership is not without its difficulties, which include issues relating to worker rights and environmental sustainability as well as disruptions caused by advances in technology. The ability of firms and politicians to handle these difficulties while simultaneously ensuring that trading practices conform with labor rights and fair employment standards is essential to the success of job creation efforts that are driven by economic exchanges. To make the most of the mutually beneficial economic link that exists between trading and job creation as the world economy continues to change, it is vital to have a solid understanding of the complex interaction that exists between the two.

2.4 Impact on Infrastructure Development

Infrastructure pertaining to transport:

The uninterrupted flow of products and services requires transportation infrastructure that is both reliable and effective. Transportation infrastructure, such as roads, bridges, ports, and airports, must be built, maintained, and expanded in order to accommodate the needs of commercial operations like trading. When there is a rise in the volume of trade, governments and commercial entities frequently make investments in extending and modernizing these facilities so that they can handle higher volumes of cargo movement. In addition, the requirement to make commercial transactions easier has been a driving force behind the growth of contemporary logistics centers and intermodal transportation hubs.

Facilities for Transporting Goods via Sea:

Ports serve as the entry points for international trade, and the capacity of such ports has a direct bearing on the volume and efficiency of that trade. Ports frequently go through periods of major growth and modernization so that they can fulfill the requirements of global trade. This includes making the channels deeper, increasing the space available for storing containers, and implementing new technologies to optimize the handling of goods and ensure its safety. The ability of a nation to compete effectively on the international market is directly correlated to the quality of its port infrastructure.

Infrastructure Relating to Telecommunications:

When it comes to the timely exchange of information and the administration of trade activities, effective communication is absolutely necessary. Investments in the infrastructure of telecommunications are being driven by the expansion of international trade. These investments include the development of high-speed internet networks, fiber-optic cables, and satellite systems. These advancements make communication in real time possible, as well as digital transactions and the administration of supply chains remotely.

Infrastructure for Energy Supply:

Energy sources that are both dependable and plentiful are required in order to sustain industrial output and commercial endeavors. The establishment of energy infrastructure, such as power plants, refineries, and distribution networks, can be impacted by commercial activity. In order to maintain a reliable and cost-effective energy supply, the nation's energy infrastructure must keep pace with the expansion of economic activities that are driven by trade.

Utilities Serving the Public:

It is essential for individuals and companies alike to have access to clean water, sanitary facilities, and waste management services. Trading activities have an effect on the creation and upkeep of public utilities, as increased economic growth frequently necessitates the expansion of these services to accommodate a growing population and industrial base.

Infrastructure at the Customs Border and Related Facilities:

Trade cannot take place without hassle-free and timely passage through international borders. It is absolutely necessary to make investments in border facilities and customs infrastructure in order to hasten the movement of goods, lessen the likelihood of trade bottlenecks, and improve the overall environment for trade. Trade-related delays and expenses can be greatly reduced by utilizing contemporary border facilities that are outfitted with cutting-edge technology and have procedures that have been streamlined.

Industrial Zones and Special Economic Zones: What They Are and Why They Exist

Trade promotion and the construction of economic zones, both industrial and special, frequently go hand in hand with one another. These regions provide incentives to entice direct foreign investment and to make it easier for businesses to produce items for export, respectively. For the purposes of supporting manufacturing and other activities connected to trade, the construction of infrastructure within these zones is necessary.

The development of the economy and the infrastructure of the region:

Localized or corridor-specific economic expansion can be fueled by increased levels of trade activity. As a direct consequence of this, these regions may undergo major infrastructure development, which may include the establishment of new highways, railroads, and industrial parks. The expansion of regional infrastructure can, in turn, help local economies and bring about improvements in living conditions.

Although commercial activities do help to advance the construction of physical infrastructure, the relationship is not one-sided. A necessary prerequisite for profitable trade is the existence of adequate infrastructure. The cost of conducting business is lowered, the movement of commodities is facilitated, and the competitiveness of firms in the global market is increased when infrastructure is efficient, well-maintained, and in good repair. Inadequate infrastructure, on the other hand, might serve as a barrier to trade, resulting in inefficiencies, delays, and increased prices.

Chapter 3

Stock Markets and Capital Formation

The process of capital formation, which is the mobilization of savings and investments for the purpose of engaging in economically productive activities, is significantly influenced by the stock markets. These markets provide as a platform for businesses to generate cash by issuing stocks to the general public, enabling investors to take part in ownership, and facilitating the exchange of ownership holdings in enterprises. This all-encompassing investigation digs into the complex web of connections that exist between stock markets and the process of capital formation. It investigates the ways in which stock markets contribute to economic expansion, encourage innovation, and provide chances for individuals to amass wealth.

1. **Comprehending the Process of Capital Formation:**

Explanation of the Concept and Its Importance:
The process of amassing a variety of assets, both tangible and intangible, for the aim of driving the expansion and improvement of an economy is known as capital formation. It is a key procedure that enables corporations and governments to generate the funds necessary for investment in a variety of initiatives and endeavors, and it is essential to the process.

Formations of Different Kinds of Capital:

1. **Gross Capital Formation:** This refers to the overall investment that has been made in an economy, which might come from either the public or private sector.
2. **Net Capital Formation:** This determines the difference between the capital stock at the end of the current year and the end of the preceding year, taking into account any depreciation that may have occurred.
3. **Human Capital Formation:** This comprises making investments in education, training, and the development of skills, all of which increase the workforce's potential for increased productivity and earnings.

II. The Role of the Stock Market in the Formation of Capital:
Initial Public Offerings are abbreviated as IPOs

The initial public offerings (IPOs) that take place on stock exchanges provide businesses with a venue for the raising of cash. When a firm decides to sell its shares to the public for the first time, investors can buy those shares from the company. The monies that are created by initial public offerings (IPOs) are put to use for a variety of goals, including debt reduction, research and development, and business expansion.

Additional Products and Services:

Secondary offers allow companies to issue extra shares, which they can then sell to investors in order to raise further capital. These offers may provide a route for further capital formation and may take the form of follow-on stock offerings, rights issues, or convertible securities.

Capital Contributions:

Equity finance, which is typically connected to stock markets, enables businesses to raise capital through the sale of ownership holdings in the form of common stocks and preferred stocks. Investors put up the money in exchange for a piece of the company's ownership and, if things go well, a cut of its future income.

III. Economic Expansion and the Accumulation of Capital:
Investing in Assets That Will Produce a Return:

The accumulation of capital enables a company to make investments in productive assets such as equipment, technological advancements, and physical infrastructure. As a result, this leads to an increase in production capacity, which in turn boosts efficiency and promotes economic growth.

Creating New Jobs:

New employment opportunities emerge as a natural byproduct of a company's efforts to grow and fund new ventures. The production of capital results in an increased demand for labor, which in turn contributes to a reduction in unemployment and an improvement in living conditions.

The Development of Infrastructure:

The process of capital formation is used by governments in order to invest in important infrastructure projects such as roads, bridges, utilities, and public transportation networks. These developments both encourage economic expansion and make residents' quality of life significantly better.

Investigation and Experimentation:

The accumulation of capital is necessary for carrying out research and development operations, which are the engines of innovation and technical advancement. This, in turn, results in the development of new goods, services, and businesses across a variety of sectors.

IV. Creativity and the Accumulation of Capital:
Financial Support for Research and Development (R&D):

Companies are able to gain access to large funds, which can then be used to support research and development projects thanks to the stock markets. This money is essential for innovation, which, in turn, improves the chances of growth and competitiveness for firms.

Ecosystem for New Businesses:

Capital generation through the stock markets is essential for emerging growth corporations as well as start-up businesses. These companies frequently do not have access to traditional sources of finance; hence, stock markets offer a suitable venue for them to raise capital and stimulate innovation in order to compensate for this gap.

Both technology and biotechnology will be discussed.

Both the technology and biotechnology industries are extremely reliant on the generation of capital through the stock markets. These areas of research have sparked a revolution in their respective industries and opened the door for the development of ground-breaking goods and services.

V. The Accumulation of Wealth and the Stock Markets:

The act of diversifying:

Individuals have the opportunity to diversify their portfolios by investing in stocks, which offers them with this possibility. Individuals have the ability to diversify their risk and perhaps amass money over time through the use of stock markets, which provide a diverse array of investment possibilities.

Increase in Value of Capital:

Historically speaking, the long-term performance of stock prices has indicated that there is the possibility for financial appreciation. The buildup of wealth is possible for those investors who retain stocks since growing stock prices are beneficial to those investors.

Obtaining Income and Dividends:

There are a variety of companies that offer dividends, which provide shareholders with a source of consistent income. This revenue has the potential to be reinvested, which will further boost the creation of wealth.

VI. Difficulties and Things to Think About:

Volatility of the Market:

The stock market is prone to having periods that are marked by high levels of volatility and unpredictability. Price swings can have an effect on investor confidence and can sway the decisions investors make, which may have a knock-on effect on capital formation.

Regulation of the Market:

Effective regulatory oversight is necessary for protecting the integrity of stock markets and maintaining their stability. It is absolutely necessary to have robust regulatory frameworks in order to keep the confidence of investors and guard against market manipulation and fraud.

Inclusion in Financial Matters:

It is essential to make sure that a larger portion of the public is able to engage in stock markets since they provide opportunities for the acquisition of wealth. The democratization of access to stock markets can be assisted by programs that promote financial inclusion and investor education.

Liquidity on the Market:

The level of liquidity present in stock markets is absolutely necessary for the effective operation of the capital formation process. Trading can be hampered and it becomes more difficult for investors to enter or leave positions when there is insufficient liquidity.

The development of capital is facilitated in large part by the stock markets, which are an essential component of this process. Stock markets play a pivotal role in the acceleration of economic growth, the promotion of innovation, and the provision of chances for the accumulation of personal wealth.

The stock markets offer businesses a mechanism of raising funds for the purpose of making profitable investments. These methods include initial public offerings, secondary offers, and equity financing. In turn, the formation of capital leads to economic growth, the creation of new jobs, the expansion of existing infrastructure, and innovation.

Although the link between stock markets and the production of capital is mutually beneficial, it is not without its difficulties. These difficulties include the volatility of the market, the necessity of financial inclusion, and regulatory considerations. A well-functioning stock market, supported by efficient regulation and investor education, has the potential to be a powerful instrument for driving economic growth and fostering wealth accumulation, which, in the end, is to the benefit of both firms and individuals.

3.1 The Function of Stock Markets

stock markets, also known as equity markets or bourses, play in the operation of modern economies cannot be overstated. Stock markets are sometimes referred to as the "backbone" of the global financial system. These markets provide as a venue for the purchase and sale of ownership interests in publicly traded corporations, thereby easing the process of allocating capital, encouraging investment, and fostering the growth of personal wealth. In this extensive investigation, we dig into the numerous functions of stock markets, investigating how they contribute to economic growth, encourage the production of capital, promote liquidity, and facilitate risk management.

1. **The Accumulation of Capital:**
   The Initial Market:
   The initial public offerings (IPOs) of firms are made possible, thanks to the role that stock markets serve as key facilitators in the primary market. When a company decides to go public, it will sell its shares to the general public. Investors will then buy these shares, giving the company with capital that may be used for

a variety of goals, such as business growth, research and development, and the repayment of debt. The initial stage of the capital formation process is known as the primary market, and the stock markets are the major means by which businesses can gain access to this essential source of money.

Markets that are Secondary:

The secondary market, which is where shares that have already been issued can be bought and sold, is also very crucial for the process of capital formation. Secondary offers, also known as follow-on stock offerings, rights issues, and convertible instruments, are all different ways that businesses have the opportunity to obtain extra capital. These options provide businesses with the opportunity to grow their operations, reduce their debt, or invest in new projects.

Capital Contributions:

The growth of equity finance is made possible by stock markets, which enable businesses to acquire capital through the sale of ownership holdings in the form of common and preferred stocks. Investors put up the money in exchange for a piece of the company's ownership and, if things go well, a cut of its future income. This method of equity financing helps to boost capital creation by giving businesses access to the resources they require in order to make investments and expand.

2. **The Provision of Liquidity:**

Liquidity on the Market:

By offering a venue for the purchase and sale of shares, stock markets contribute to an increase in the overall market's liquidity. As a result of this liquidity, investors are able to enter and exit positions with relative ease, and it is also easy to convert ownership stakes into cash. The ability of stock markets to maintain a high level of market liquidity is essential to their operations because it ensures that there is a market in which buyers and sellers can trade securities in an effective manner.

The Discovery of Prices:

Price discovery is the process of discovering the fair market value of various securities, and the stock markets play an important role in this process. The fluctuation of stock prices, which is caused by the competition between supply and demand, is a reflection of the general agreement among investors regarding the worth of a company's shares. The accurate discovery of prices is critical for investors, as it assists them in making educated judgments regarding their investments.

Effective Utilization of Financial Resources:

The efficient distribution of capital is made possible by stock markets, which enable investors to channel their money into businesses that have a strong future and significant room for expansion. This procedure makes it possible for capital to flow to enterprises that are best able to put it to use, so contributing to the growth and effectiveness of the economy as a whole.

3. **Potential Opportunities for Investment:**
The act of diversifying:
Investors have the chance to diversify their portfolios of investments through the use of stock markets. The practice of distributing investments across a number of different asset classes, sectors, and industries is what is meant by the term "diversification."

This lowers the risk that is associated with having all of one's assets concentrated in a single investment. Investors are able to successfully control risk thanks to the extensive range of investment possibilities that are made available by stock markets.

Increase in Value of Capital:
Historically speaking, the long-term performance of stock prices has indicated that there is the possibility for financial appreciation. The buildup of wealth is possible for those investors who retain stocks since growing stock prices are beneficial to those investors. Investing in the stock market allows individuals the chance to enhance their wealth over time through a phenomenon known as capital appreciation, which is an essential component of the market.

Profits from Dividends
A significant number of stocks routinely distribute dividends to their shareholders. Investors who get dividend income have a source of consistent income at their disposal, which can be of particular use to individuals who are looking for a reliable cash flow stream. This revenue has the potential to be reinvested, which will further boost the creation of wealth.

4. **Management of the Risks:**
Avoiding Risk:
The stock market provides chances for hedging, which enables investors to shield their portfolios from the impact of unfavorable price swings. Taking positions in the market that are designed to reduce exposure to risk by offsetting prospective losses is what hedging entails. For instance, investors can hedge against negative price movements by purchasing futures contracts and options on futures contracts.

A Diversification of Risks:
One of the most fundamental techniques for risk management is diversification, which is made possible by stock markets. Investors can lower the risk associated with their investments in individual firms or industries by maintaining a broad portfolio of stock holdings. The impact of bad performance on a single investment will have less of an effect on the portfolio as a whole.

5. **Innovation and the Promotion of Economic Growth:**
Investing in Assets That Will Produce a Return:

The production of capital through the use of stock markets makes it possible for enterprises to make investments in productive assets such as machinery, technology, and infrastructure.

As a result, this leads to an increase in production capacity, which in turn boosts efficiency and promotes economic growth.

Creating New Jobs:

New employment opportunities emerge as a natural byproduct of a company's efforts to grow and fund new ventures. The production of capital results in an increased demand for labor, which in turn contributes to a reduction in unemployment and an improvement in living conditions.

The Development of Infrastructure:

The process of capital formation is used by governments in order to invest in important infrastructure projects such as roads, bridges, utilities, and public transportation networks. These developments both encourage economic expansion and make residents' quality of life significantly better.

Investigation and Experimentation:

The accumulation of capital is necessary for carrying out research and development operations, which are the engines of innovation and technical advancement. This, in turn, results in the development of new goods, services, and businesses across a variety of sectors.

6. **Difficulties and Things to Think About:**

Volatility of the Market:

The stock market is prone to having periods that are marked by high levels of volatility and unpredictability. Price swings can have an effect on investor confidence and can sway the decisions investors make, which can possibly have repercussions for capital formation and investment strategies.

Regulation of the Market:

Effective regulatory oversight is necessary for protecting the integrity of stock markets and maintaining their stability. It is absolutely necessary to have robust regulatory frameworks in order to keep the confidence of investors and guard against market manipulation and fraud.

Inclusion in Financial Matters:

It is essential to guarantee that a larger portion of the public is able to engage in stock markets because these markets provide chances for the accumulation of wealth as well as investment options. The democratization of access to stock markets can be assisted by programs that promote financial inclusion and investor education.

Liquidity on the Market:

The existence of a liquid market for stocks is essential to the effective operation of the processes of capital formation and investment. Trading can be hampered and it becomes more difficult for investors to enter or leave positions when there is insufficient liquidity.

The stock market is a fundamental component of modern economies because it performs key activities such as promoting liquidity, supporting capital formation, facilitating risk management, and contributing to economic expansion and innovation. Companies are able to raise funds for investment, expansion, and development through the use of stock markets, which include both primary and secondary markets. These markets also provide opportunity for investors to diversify their portfolios, create wealth through capital appreciation and dividend income, and successfully manage risk, all of which can be accomplished through the use of these markets.

Even though stock markets are essential, they are not without their share of difficulties. Some of these difficulties include the volatility of the market, the necessity of financial inclusion, and regulatory concerns. A well-functioning stock market that is supported by good regulation and investor education has the potential to be a powerful weapon for driving economic growth, fostering the accumulation of wealth, and ensuring that money is allocated effectively to support innovation and development.

3.2 Capital Formation and Investment

The generation of new capital and the investment of existing capital are two interdependent pillars that support economic expansion and development. The process of accumulating financial and physical assets for productive purposes is referred to as capital creation. On the other hand, investment refers to the deployment of these assets in order to generate income and contribute to the expansion of the economy. Together, they contribute to the advancement of the economy, the creation of new job opportunities, and the improvement of living conditions. Within the scope of this in-depth study, we investigate the ideas of capital formation and investment, as well as the significance of each, the different forms that it can take, and the essential function that it serves within the economy of the entire world.

1. **Comprehending the Process of Capital Formation:**

In this sense

The act of accumulating savings and investments for the purpose of engaging in productive economic activity is referred to as capital formation. It entails laying aside a portion of one's income or wealth in order to generate additional capital, which can then be utilized for a variety of objectives, including the expansion of an existing firm, the building of new infrastructure, and research and development.

Formations of Different Kinds of Capital:

1. **Gross Capital Formation:** This refers to the sum of all investments made in an economy, including those made by the public sector as well as those made by the private sector.

2. **Net Capital Formation:** This calculation takes into account any depreciation or wear and tear that has occurred on existing capital stock. As a result, it provides a measure of capital growth that is more accurate.

3. **Human Capital Formation:** This sort of capital formation refers to investments made in education, training, and the development of skills with the goal of increasing the workforce's potential for both increased productivity and increased earnings.

II. The Importance of the Accumulation of Capital:

Growth of the Economy:

The accumulation of new capital is one of the primary engines that propel economic expansion. It gives companies the opportunity to invest in brand new projects, boost their production capacity, and modernize existing infrastructure, all of which contribute to the expansion of the economy.

Creating New Jobs:

The process of accumulating money ultimately results in a rise in investment, which, in turn, results in the production of employment openings. Companies that are developing and investing in new businesses will need a larger workforce to support their expansion and new business endeavors.

The Development of Infrastructure:

The accumulation of capital is absolutely necessary for the development of infrastructure, such as roadways, bridges, utility networks, and public transportation systems. Investing in infrastructure may improve quality of life, cut costs for transportation, and stimulate regional economic growth.

Investigation and Experimentation:

The funding of research and development (R&D) activities, which are the engines of innovation and technological advancement, is made possible by investments in capital formation. Investing in research and development can result in the production of new goods, services, and even entire industries.

III. Different Methods of Accumulating Capital:

The Accumulation of Actual Capital:

The term "physical capital" refers to immovable assets that can be seen and touched, such as machines, tools, buildings, and infrastructure. The construction of physical capital entails making investments in the aforementioned assets with the goal of enhancing production capacities and fostering economic expansion.

The Accumulation of Financial Capital:

The accumulation of financial assets, such as savings, investments, and other financial instruments, is what is meant by the term "financial capital formation." This particular method of accumulating money is essential for both individuals and organizations that want to amass wealth for a variety of reasons, including retiring, furthering their education, and growing their company.

The Formation of Human Capital:

The workforce's knowledge, skills, and capacities all make up what economists refer to as "human capital." Increasing one's human capital through investments in education, training, and the development of skills leads to improved levels of both production and earning potential. It is essential to both one's personal growth and the advancement of economic conditions.

IV. The Importance of Investments:

In this sense

The process of allocating capital or other resources with the intention of generating revenue or accomplishing other financial objectives is known as investment. It encompasses a wide range of investments, including monetary investments, real estate investments, company investments, and investments in one's own personal growth.

Various Forms of Investments:

1. **Financial Investment:** This refers to the process of purchasing financial assets such as stocks, bonds, and mutual funds.
2. **Real Estate Investment:** Involves the purchase and management of properties, including residential and commercial real estate. This type of investment can be profitable.
3. **Investment in the Business:** This term refers to the deployment of funds for the purpose of expanding the business, conducting research and development, and meeting other operational requirements.
4. **Human Capital Investment:** This refers to the process of enhancing one's personal earning potential through education, training, and skill development.

The Significance of Investing in:

Investors are rewarded with both income and appreciation of their initial investment.

Fosters creativity as well as the development of innovative new products and services.

Encourages the formation of new jobs and the development of new employment prospects.

Contributes to the increased financial security and stability of enterprises and individuals.

V. Financial Market Investments:

Investment in the Financial Markets:

Individuals and institutions have the opportunity to invest in a variety of financial assets, including stocks, bonds, commodities, and currencies, through the use of the platform that is provided by financial markets. Investors are given the opportunity to allocate cash and develop diversified portfolios thanks to these markets.

Investment in the Stock Market:

Investors have the chance to acquire ownership holdings in publicly traded companies through participation in stock markets, which are often referred to as equity markets. An investment in stocks offers the potential for financial appreciation, dividend payments, and a share in the profits of a successful firm.

Investing in the Bond Market:

The bond market offers options for investing in fixed-income instruments, such as bonds issued by corporations and governments. Bonds are investments that provide investors with periodic interest payments in addition to the return of the principal amount when the bond matures.

Investment in a Mutual Fund :

Mutual funds are investment vehicles that combine the capital contributed by a number of different participants in order to purchase a diverse portfolio of stocks, bonds, and other assets. They provide investors a diversified portfolio as well as management from trained professionals.

VI. Factors That Have an Impact on Investment:

Conditions in the Economy:

The state of the economy as a whole, which can be broken down into individual components such as inflation, interest rates, and GDP growth, has a substantial impact on the choices that are made about investments. Investing is typically encouraged when an economy is both stable and rising.

Tolerance for Risk:

Investors, both individual and institutional, have various comfort levels with risk, which impacts the investments they choose to make. Investments with a higher risk might potentially yield larger returns; however, these returns come with increased market volatility and the possibility of a loss.

The Sense of the Market:

The emotion of investors, which can be strongly impacted by the news, movements in the market, and public perception, can have a considerable impact on investment decisions. Investing decisions can be influenced by a person's feelings as well as their understanding of market psychology.

Environment Subject to Regulation:

Investment decisions are susceptible to being impacted by governmental rules, tax policies, and legal frameworks. The presence of favorable regulatory conditions may serve to attract investment, whilst the presence of adverse regulatory conditions may serve to discourage investment.

The creation of new capital and the investing of existing capital are the fundamental activities that underpin economic expansion and development. The increase of production capacity, the creation of new jobs, the development of new infrastructure, and the introduction of innovative new ideas all require the formation of capital, which includes physical capital, financial capital, and human capital. Individuals and businesses have the opportunity to allocate capital for the purpose of income production and the accumulation of wealth when they participate in one of the many kinds of investment.

Investors have access to a wide variety of investment options through the financial markets, which include stock and bond markets. These markets enable investors to take part in the expansion of the economy and the success of businesses. Numerous aspects, such as the state of the economy, one's level of comfort with taking risks, the current mood of the market, and the policies now in place, all play a part in determining investment choices.

Not only are the development of capital and the investing of funds economic processes, but they are also tactics that individuals and businesses can employ to contribute to their own financial well-being and prosperity. In order to make educated decisions that are in line with one's financial goals and desires, it is essential to have a solid understanding of the dynamics of capital production and investment. This, in turn, will contribute to one's own financial stability as well as to the expansion of the economy as a whole.

3.3 Role in Entrepreneurship and Business Growth

The generation of new capital and the investing of existing capital are two essential components of entrepreneurial endeavors and the expansion of existing businesses. These components encourage innovation, ensure access to critical resources, and pave the way for further growth. To fuel their operations, business owners and aspiring business owners rely on having access to finance, which can come from personal savings, investments from outside sources, or loans. This article digs into the crucial roles that capital formation and investment play in the ecosystem of entrepreneurship, illuminating how these factors make it possible for enterprises to start up and flourish.

1. **Methods of Financial Support for New Businesses:**
   Initial Investment:
   Seed cash is frequently required by entrepreneurs in order to develop their novel business concepts into profitable enterprises. The initial funding can come from personal savings, from friends and family, or from investors known as angels. This acts as the initial capital that allows entrepreneurs to produce prototypes, carry out market research, and establish the framework for their businesses.
   The term "Venture Capital"
   When companies reach a certain level of maturity, they may decide to go for venture capital, which can be obtained from investment firms or professional venture capitalists. Injections of venture capital are essential for growing a business to a larger scale, penetrating new markets, and bolstering efforts to conduct research and development. These investments typically come with the assistance of knowledgeable investors who can offer advice and expertise.
   The term "private equity"
   Private equity can be a significant source of capital for companies that have

already achieved some level of success. Private equity firms make investments in companies with the goal of assisting those companies in achieving growth and improving their operations. These investments are often put toward business expansions, mergers & acquisitions, and strategic initiatives.

2. **Stepping Up the Pace of Business Growth:**
R&D stands for "research and development."
The accumulation of capital and the making of investments are both essential components of R&D endeavors. Innovating, creating new items, and improving existing services are all ways that businesses put these capital to use. Investing in research and development boosts a company's competitiveness, encourages growth, and enables it to maintain its lead in markets that are always shifting.

Expansion of the Market:
Investment is critical to the expansion of a company because it enables the company to acquire the resources necessary to penetrate new markets. The expansion of a company's operations into new geographic regions, the pursuit of new consumer demographics, or the introduction of new product lines are all activities that call for financial investment.

Technology and the Infrastructure Behind It:
The accumulation of capital is absolutely necessary for the construction and improvement of infrastructure, which includes the establishment of production facilities, supply chain networks, and digital technology systems. These expenditures improve operational efficiency and make it possible for enterprises to fulfill the needs of an expanding customer base.

The Development of Human Capital:
It is essential for the growth of a company to make investments in the education and development of its workforce, as well as in the recruitment and retention of top talent. Employees that are knowledgeable, skilled, and well-trained contribute to greater production and innovation, which ultimately drives the success of a firm.

3. **Providing Assistance to New Businesses and Promoting Innovation:**
The Difference Between Incubators and Accelerators
Early-stage enterprises might benefit from the funding, coaching, and tools that are made available by startup incubators and accelerators, which are frequently financed by investors and venture capitalists. These programs assist new business ventures in overcoming the obstacles associated with starting their own businesses, which in turn speeds up their growth and improves their chances of being successful.

Incubators of New Ideas:
The production of new capital is inextricably linked to the establishment of innovation hubs. These hubs serve as meeting places for new enterprises, entrepreneurs, and established companies to interact and share ideas. These nodes

provide a setting that is receptive to new ideas and access to various options for financial investment.

Financial Support for Creative Concepts:

In order to bring their ideas to life as profitable businesses, innovative business-people frequently need financial backing. Investors and venture capitalists play a critical role in enabling early-stage innovators to commercialize their ideas by providing the required financial backing and enabling them to bring their ideas to market.

4. **Reducing the Impact of Risk and Uncertainty:**

   The act of diversifying:

   Entrepreneurs and businesses utilize investment diversification as a risk management approach to distribute risk across a variety of assets and initiatives in order to reduce overall exposure to risk. Having a diversified portfolio of investments can assist reduce the adverse effects of prospective losses and uncertainties, hence increasing the likelihood of sustained growth for a company.

   A Availability of Working Capital:

   It is essential for companies to have adequate working capital, which refers to the capital that is readily available for day-to-day operations. It assists in the management of short-term financial needs, the payment of bills, and the maintenance of liquidity throughout periods of fluctuation and uncertainty.

5. **Obstacles and Things to Take Into Account:**

Preparedness for Investment:

In order to entice possible investors, entrepreneurs need to ensure that their businesses are "investment ready." To accomplish this, you will need to create an enticing business strategy, articulate your value proposition, and have a thorough understanding of the dynamics of the market.

Relations with Investors:

Maintaining a fruitful connection with investors and other stakeholders requires having strong investor relations in place at all times. To keep the confidence of investors, it is essential to maintain transparency, clear communication, and fulfillment of agreements.

Finding the Right Mix of Debt and Equity:

When it comes to capital development, entrepreneurs have the responsibility of striking a balance between the use of debt and equity. High amounts of debt can put a strain on a company's finances, and excessive equity dilution can have an effect on ownership and control of the company.

Administration of Risk:

An important factor to take into account is how to reduce the dangers connected to financial investing. In order to address potential difficulties, it is necessary to do an accurate risk analysis, diversify one's holdings, and plan for various contingencies.

The development of capital and the investment of that capital are essential components of entrepreneurial endeavors and the expansion of existing businesses. They give the financial resources essential to turn creative ideas into thriving businesses, encourage research and development, and make it easier to expand into new markets. These processes also assist business owners and entrepreneurs in navigating risks and uncertainties, which ensures the businesses' continued viability and success over the long term.

The formation of capital and the making of investments are two fundamental tenets that are necessary for the healthy growth of entrepreneurial endeavors, as well as for the stimulation of economic growth and the production of new employment opportunities. In the context of the entrepreneurial ecosystem, the processes of capital formation and investment play a dynamic and mutually reinforcing function. This helps to foster an environment in which new enterprises, established businesses, and innovative ideas can thrive.

3.4 IPOs and Corporate Finance

Initial Public Offerings and Capital Infusion:

Initial public offerings (IPOs) provide businesses with the opportunity to get significant funding from the public markets. These funds can be essential for corporate financing, allowing a firm to finance a variety of projects such as expanding operations, investing in research and development, lowering debt, or pursuing strategic acquisitions. They can also be used for other purposes. An initial public offering (IPO) can give a firm with the injection of capital that can provide the required financial resources to drive the company's growth and development.

Gaining Entry to the Public Markets:

A company can acquire access to the huge pool of cash that is available in the public stock markets by going public through the process of an initial public offering (IPO). This access can be especially useful for businesses who are looking to finance ambitious initiatives or capitalize on growth prospects that may be out of reach for them if they rely solely on private investors or debt financing.

Increasing the Value of the Corporation:

An initial public offering (IPO) can result in a considerable boost in the worth of a firm. Being publicly traded frequently brings with it enhanced transparency, trustworthiness, and visibility, all of which contribute to this phenomenon. Not only does a higher valuation entice possible investors, but it also has the potential to act as collateral for future funding and expansion attempts.

Diversification of Investments and Access to Capital Markets for Shareholders:

Existing shareholders, such as the company's founders and early investors, have the option to realize the value of their holdings through the sale of shares to the general public during an initial public offering (IPO). This offers liquidity to stakeholders, some of whom may have a significant portion of their capital locked up in the company. As a result, these individuals are able to diversify their investment portfolios and lower the amount of risk they are exposed to.

Transparency and the Governance of Corporations:

Before a company can become publicly traded, it must satisfy stringent regulatory and reporting requirements. The company's reputation, trustworthiness, and attractiveness to investors may all benefit from placing a greater emphasis on transparency and corporate governance. Because it fosters confidence in the company and contributes to its continued viability over the long term, it is an essential component of corporate finance.

Chapter 4

Trading and Financial Inclusion

Trading, which encompasses a wide variety of different financial activities, plays an important role as a driver of economic expansion and development. In recent years, the integration of trading platforms and technologies has played a crucial role in increasing financial inclusion and giving individuals and communities access to financial services and markets. This has occurred as a result of the provision that these technologies have made possible. This in-depth investigation delves into the complex relationship that exists between trading and financial inclusion. It examines how developments in trading technologies, regulatory frameworks, and educational initiatives are enabling individuals, particularly those living in underserved and marginalized communities, to take part in the economy on a global scale.

1. Comprehending the Meaning of Financial Inclusion:

Explanation of the Concept and Its Importance:
The term "financial inclusion" refers to the ease with which individuals and enterprises, especially those who are excluded from the traditional banking system, can gain access to and make use of various forms of financial assistance. By offering chances for the creation of wealth and the accumulation of assets, it plays a significant part in the advancement of economic development, the alleviation of poverty, and the promotion of social fairness.

Included in this category are the following aspects:

1. **Access to Banking Services:** This refers to having the ability to utilize fundamental banking services such as savings accounts, credit facilities, and payment systems.
2. Access to financing In order to support a variety of economic activities and investment efforts, individuals and businesses need to have access to financing that is within their price range.

3. **Insurance and Risk Management:** Having access to various insurance products is necessary in order to effectively manage risks and shield individuals, corporations, and other organizations from potential financial vulnerabilities.

4. **Opportunities to Invest:** Individuals now have the ability to increase their wealth and engage in the financial markets thanks to increased access to investment platforms and markets.

II. The Importance of Commercial Activity to Financial Inclusion:

Access to Markets Being Made More Easily Available:

Trading platforms, both traditional and digital, have been essential in the democratization of access to financial markets in recent years. Individuals are now able to participate in a wider variety of financial instruments and investment opportunities because to the proliferation of digital marketplaces, mobile applications, and online trading platforms, which have drastically lowered the entrance barriers.

Providing Assistance with Investment Education:

Trading has made it easier to educate people about investments and increase their financial literacy, which has provided individuals with the knowledge and tools they need to make educated decisions about their investments. Individuals have been given the ability to understand difficult financial concepts and methods as a result of the proliferation of educational tools, webinars, and online tutorials. This has helped to cultivate a culture of informed decision-making.

Microfinance and micro investing: a comparative study

Individuals who have little resources are now able to gain access to small-scale investment opportunities because to the proliferation of microfinance and microinvesting programs that have been made possible by trading platforms. Individuals are given the opportunity to deposit little sums of money in diversified portfolios through micro-investing platforms, which are typically made available through mobile applications. This encourages a culture of saving money and investing it.

Gaining Access to International Markets:

Trading technology have made it possible for people living in underserved and rural regions to access global financial markets. As a result, these individuals now have access to a wider variety of investment opportunities that go beyond the scope of their own local economies. Individuals' financial horizons have been enlarged as a result of the globalization of investment possibilities, which has contributed to the development of a sense of financial empowerment and inclusion.

III. Financial Inclusion and the Impact of Digital Transformation:

Banking and Payment Solutions on Mobile Devices:

Financial inclusion has been completely transformed as a result of the integration of mobile banking and payment solutions with trade platforms, in particular in geographical areas with restricted access to traditional banking infrastructure. Individuals are now able to execute financial transactions, monitor investments, and obtain market information while they are on the move thanks to the proliferation of mobile-based trading applications and payment gateways.

Innovations in Financial Technology

Fintech innovations, such as blockchain technology, digital wallets, and peer-to-peer lending platforms, have played a game-changing role in expanding access to financial services and helping more people participate in the financial system. Because of these developments, financial procedures have been expedited, transaction costs have been decreased, and access to financial services has been expanded, particularly for underprivileged communities and populations.

Frameworks for Regulatory Compliance and the Protection of Consumers:

Regulatory frameworks that control trading activities have developed throughout time to ensure the protection of consumers, transparency in market operations, and the integrity of markets. Strong regulatory frameworks inspire individuals' trust and confidence, which in turn encourages individuals' engagement in various forms of trade and in the financial markets.

IV. Obstacles and Things to Take Into Account:

The Digital Divide and Other Barriers Caused by Technology:

Individuals living in distant and underserved communities continue to face difficulties in terms of internet connectivity, technological literacy, and access to digital equipment. This digital gap is a key obstacle to financial inclusion. To close this gap will take coordinated efforts from governmental bodies, non-governmental groups, and educational establishments.

Concerns Regarding Compliance with Regulations and Safety:

For the purpose of creating trust and confidence among individuals who participate in online trading activities, ensuring regulatory compliance and resolving security concerns are essential components. In order to protect the interests of traders and investors, it is vital to put in place effective cybersecurity protections, data protection mechanisms, and regulatory compliance frameworks.

Education and Training in Financial Matters:

It is vital to promote financial literacy and education campaigns in order to equip individuals with the knowledge and skills necessary to manage the intricacies of financial markets. This will enable individuals to take control of their financial futures. Programs and workshops for investment education, as well as easily accessible educational resources, can all play an important part in the process of encouraging informed decision-making and responsible financial conduct.

Trading, with its transformative potential, has emerged as a key enabler of financial inclusion. Trading gives individuals and communities access to financial services, investment possibilities, and global markets. This is especially beneficial for individuals and communities located in underserved and marginalized regions. The integration of digital technology, advancements in fintech, and educational programs has played a crucial role in the promotion of economic growth as well as the empowerment of individuals in their financial situations. To realize the full potential of trading in promoting financial inclusion and creating a more inclusive and equitable global economy, concerted efforts from governments, financial institutions, and technological innovators are essential. Challenges related to the digital divide, regulatory compliance, and financial literacy continue to persist.

4.1 The Link Between Trading and Financial Inclusion

The recent years have seen a substantial shift in the global financial environment, which has been driven by the expansion of trading platforms and the development of digital technology. This transition has not only brought about a sea change in the manner in which financial markets function, but it has also been an essential factor in the advancement of financial inclusion. Individuals, particularly those living in underserved and marginalized communities, can be given more agency through trading in its many guises since it gives them access to investment opportunities, financial services, and global markets. This is especially true for people living in communities that have historically been disadvantaged. Trading activities have been shown to foster economic empowerment, enhanced financial literacy, and facilitated the integration of individuals into the global financial ecosystem. The purpose of this in-depth analysis is to investigate the complex relationship that exists between trading and financial inclusion, with the goal of highlighting the ways in which trading activities have done so.

1. **Comprehending the Meaning of Financial Inclusion:**

In terms of definition and range:

The term "financial inclusion" refers to the availability of a wide variety of financial services as well as their utilization. These services can include banking, credit, insurance, and investment options.

It aspires to promote economic development, decrease poverty, and build social fairness by supplying individuals and businesses, particularly those who are marginalized from the traditional banking system, with the tools and resources essential for financial empowerment and stability. These goals will be accomplished by giving individuals and businesses with the tools and resources necessary for financial empowerment and stability.

Included in this category are the following aspects:

1. **Access to Basic Banking Services:** This includes savings accounts, checking accounts, and payment services, which provide consumers with the ability to conveniently manage their financial operations.
2. **Credit and Lending Facilities:** Having access to credit and lending services at prices that are affordable is one of the most important things that can be done to promote a variety of economic activities, including entrepreneurship, education, and housing.

3. **Insurance and Risk Management:** The availability of insurance products assists individuals and businesses in effectively managing the risks associated with unforeseen occurrences such as illness, natural catastrophes, and accidents.

4. **Investment and Wealth Management:** Providing individuals with access to investment options and wealth management services enables them to amass assets, construct a foundation of financial security, and make plans for the future.

II. The Importance of Commercial Activity to the Provision of Financial Services:

Access to Financial Markets Being Made More Easily Available:

Trading platforms, both traditional and digital, have been crucial in expanding access to financial markets and making trading more democratic. Because of the drastically lowered entry barriers created by online trading platforms, mobile applications, and digital marketplaces, individuals from a wide range of socioeconomic backgrounds are now able to participate in a variety of investment options. These opportunities include stocks, bonds, commodities, and foreign exchange.

Enhancing Competence in Financial Matters:

The spread of financial literacy and education has been made possible by the activities of trading, which has enabled individuals to acquire the knowledge and abilities necessary to make educated judgments regarding their investments. Individuals have been given the ability to grasp the mechanics of financial markets, investing strategies, and risk management as a result of the proliferation of educational resources, seminars, and online tutorials. This has helped to cultivate a culture of informed decision-making and responsible financial conduct.

Initiatives Regarding Microfinance and Micro Investing:

Individuals who have little financial resources are now able to access chances for small-scale investments thanks to the integration of trading platforms with microfinance and microinvesting initiatives. Individuals are given the opportunity to invest modest sums of money in diversified portfolios through the use of micro-investing platforms, which may be accessed through mobile applications and digital platforms. This encourages a culture of savings and investment among neglected populations.

Finding Common Ground between Local and International Markets:

People living in distant or underdeveloped places now have access to global investment opportunities thanks to the gap that trading operations have spanned between local and global financial markets. Individuals have been given the ability to diversify their investment portfolios and reduce risk as a result of the globalization of financial markets, which has provided them with access to a wider range of asset classes and investment instruments than those available in their domestic economies.

III. Developments in Digital Technologies and Expanding Access to Financial Services:

Banking on Mobile Devices and Other Digital Payment Options:

The integration of trading platforms with mobile banking and digital payment solutions has revolutionized financial inclusion, particularly in areas with limited access to traditional banking infrastructure. This is especially true in countries where mobile banking and digital payment solutions are not widely available. Individuals now have more financial freedom and control as a result of the proliferation of mobile-based trading applications and payment gateways, which have made it possible to conduct financial transactions and investment management more efficiently and have access to real-time market information.

Innovations in Financial Technology and Other Inclusive Technologies:

Fintech developments, such as digital wallets, blockchain technology, and peer-to-peer lending platforms, have been a game-changer in the effort to expand access to financial services and increase financial inclusion.

These inclusive technologies have streamlined financial processes, reduced transaction costs, and expanded access to a wide range of financial services, including investment advisory services, automated portfolio management, and real-time market analysis. As a result, a more inclusive and accessible financial ecosystem has been fostered by these technologies.

Frameworks for Regulatory Compliance and the Protection of Consumers:

Consumer protection, market integrity, and transparency have all seen significant gains as a direct result of the establishment of robust regulatory frameworks that control trading operations. In order to promote trust and confidence among individuals and encourage their active participation in trading activities, regulatory authorities have implemented measures to ensure the security of transactions, protect investors from fraudulent activities, and uphold ethical standards within the financial markets. These measures aim to ensure the security of transactions; protect investors from fraudulent activities; and uphold ethical standards.

IV. Obstacles and Things to Take Into Account:

The Digital Divide and Other Barriers Caused by Technology:

Individuals living in distant and underserved communities continue to face challenges in terms of internet connectivity, technology knowledge, and access to digital devices. This presents a significant obstacle in the effort to promote financial inclusion. In order to effectively address these difficulties, a concerted effort is required from governments, business organizations, and educational institutions in the form of the construction of infrastructure, the implementation of digital literacy initiatives, and the expansion of cheap access to technological resources.

Concerns Regarding Compliance with Regulations and Safety:

Building trust and confidence among persons who participate in online trading activities requires first and foremost ensuring that all applicable regulations are complied with and addressing any and all security concerns. In order to protect the interests of traders and investors and mitigate the risks that are connected with data breaches, identity theft, and fraudulent activities, robust cybersecurity measures, data protection standards, and regulatory compliance frameworks are required.

Education and Training in Financial Matters:

It is essential to encourage financial literacy as well as education activities in order to provide individuals with the knowledge and abilities they need to successfully navigate the intricacies of financial markets. Investment education may play a vital role in fostering educated decision-making, responsible financial behavior, and risk management when it comes in the form of programs, workshops, and other educational tools that are easily available.

Trading and financial inclusion go hand in hand, and their mutually beneficial relationship is a crucial factor in both the economic empowerment and social growth of a community. Trading activities, with their transformative potential, have played a vital role in giving individuals and communities, particularly those in underserved and marginalized regions, with access to investment possibilities, financial services, and global financial markets. This is especially true for those in locations where access to these resources has historically been limited. An environment that promotes the financial empowerment of individuals, develops financial literacy, and facilitates the integration of individuals into the global financial ecosystem has been developed as a result of the integration of digital technologies, developments in the financial technology sector, and educational activities.

Even though issues such as the digital divide, compliance with regulations, and lack of financial literacy still exist, it is essential for governments, financial institutions, regulatory authorities, and technological innovators to work together in order to realize the full potential of trading in terms of promoting financial inclusion. Societies can work toward developing a more inclusive and equitable global economy where financial opportunities are accessible to all by continuing the development of technologies that are inclusive, implementing solid regulatory frameworks, and placing a priority on financial education.

4.2 Expanding Access to Financial Markets

Having access to financial markets is a vital factor in both the growth of the economy and the wealth of individuals. The ability of individuals and businesses to acquire cash, manage risk, invest, and plan for the future is made possible by modern economies thanks to the functioning of modern financial markets, which serve as the backbone of these economies. For the purposes of encouraging economic inclusion, lowering inequality, and improving long-term financial stability, broadening access to these markets is absolutely necessary. In this in-depth investigation, we will discuss the significance of broadening access to financial markets, the obstacles that presently stand in the way of this expansion, and the initiatives and technology that are working to make financial markets more welcoming to a wider range of people.

1. **The Importance of Having Access to the Financial Market:**
   Growth of the Economy:
   The efficient distribution of capital is impossible without the existence of financial markets. When people and companies have access to these markets, they increase their chances of securing finance for investments, growing their enterprises, and stimulating economic expansion. As a consequence of this, job possibilities are generated, which in turn encourages economic growth.
   The Accumulation of Wealth:
   Individuals have the opportunity to increase their wealth by investing in assets such as stocks, bonds, and real estate when they participate in financial markets and take advantage of the investment possibilities that are presented to them. These assets have the potential to increase in value over time, which can lead to improved financial independence and security.
   Administration of Risk:
   Having access to financial markets gives one the tools necessary to manage risk. For instance, individuals can buy insurance products to protect themselves against unforeseen occurrences, or they can diversify their financial portfolios to reduce risk. Both of these options are available to them.
   Organizing for Retirement:
   Participation in financial markets is absolutely necessary for accumulating money for retirement. Individuals can ensure that they will have sufficient financial resources during their retirement years by making investments in pension funds, retirement accounts, and other long-term savings tools.
2. **Obstacles in the Way of Access to Financial Markets:**
   Unequal Distribution of Income:
   The capacity of people with lower incomes to participate in financial markets is hindered by the existence of income gaps. It's possible that they don't have the money necessary to invest or save, leaving them open to the possibility of financial instability.
   Inadequate Knowledge of Financial Matters:
   Many people do not have the knowledge or understanding that is necessary to make decisions about their investments in an educated manner. A substantial barrier to entry into the market can be created by a lack of financial education.
   Access to Banking Services Is Restricted Because:
   Because many people in certain areas do not have access to even the most fundamental banking services, it is difficult for them to enter the financial markets. When you don't have a bank account, saving money and making investments can be difficult.
   Obstacles Presented by Regulators:
   Participation in a market can be discouraged by laws that are overly complex

and onerous. For some investors, the availability of investment options may be restricted due to the severe standards for obtaining accreditation, for instance.

3. **Expanding Market Access through Initiatives and Technologies**
Innovations in Financial Technology

Access to financial markets is undergoing a fundamental transformation as a result of financial technology, also known as fintech. The services provided by fintech companies are extremely diverse, ranging from digital banking and payment systems to robo-advisors and peer-to-peer lending platforms. Individuals are finding it less difficult to manage their own finances, make investments, and gain access to financial services as a result of technological advancements.

The Use of Mobile Banking:

People now have the ability to access their bank accounts, make payments, and even invest directly from their cellphones thanks to mobile banking. The use of mobile banking is especially advantageous in locations with restricted access to the traditional banking infrastructure.

Investing on a Small Scale:

The use of micro investing apps, which enable consumers to invest small sums of money in diversified portfolios, has been increasingly popular in recent years. This strategy reduces the difficulty of entrance for those who may not have big savings to begin with.

Platforms for Online Brokering Deals

Access to the stock and bond markets has been made more accessible as a result of the proliferation of online brokerage platforms. Individuals will have an easier time investing in securities thanks to the availability of low-cost trading and research tools provided by these platforms.

Programs to Improve Financial Literacy:

It is absolutely necessary to make efforts to increase financial education in order to broaden access to financial markets. Financial literacy programs are provided by governments, nonprofit organizations, and educational institutions to equip individuals with the knowledge necessary to make educated decisions regarding their personal finances.

4. **Obstacles and Things to Take Into Account:**

The "Digital Divide":

The digital gap is still a serious problem, particularly in areas with restricted internet access or among populations that do not own the requisite technology. In order to bridge this gap, investments need to be made in digital infrastructure, as well as universal connectivity.

Frameworks for Regulatory Compliance:

Protecting investors and preserving the integrity of the market both require regulation that is both efficient and effective. However, access can be restricted if the laws are extremely complicated or stringent. It is essential to strike a balance between providing enough protection for investors and maintaining easy access.

Instruction on Financial Matters:

It is only beneficial to increase access to financial markets if individuals have the expertise to make educated judgments about how to use such access. It is necessary to make investments in programs that educate people about finance in order to ensure that individuals can navigate these markets properly.

The process of promoting economic inclusion and encouraging financial security should begin with the expansion of access to financial markets as a crucial step. The financial markets are an extremely important component in economic expansion, the amassing of wealth, the mitigation of risk, and the planning of retirement. However, many people are unable to participate because of a variety of obstacles, such as income disparity, a lack of financial education, limited access to banking services, and regulatory restrictions.

These hurdles are being steadily eliminated as a result of developments in financial technology, mobile banking, micro investing, and programs teaching financial literacy. The revolutionary capacity of technology to make financial markets more accessible has been proved by a number of initiatives, including M-Pesa and Robinhood, amongst others.

It is necessary to address obstacles such as the digital divide, regulatory frameworks, and financial education in order to ensure the continuing growth of market access. This will help ensure that the industry continues to grow. By doing so, society can move closer to attaining the aim of making financial markets accessible to all individuals, irrespective of the level of financial expertise they possess, their level of income, or where they are located. In doing so, they have the potential to advance economic inclusion, bring about a reduction in inequality, and make a contribution to the monetary well-being of their population.

4.3 Involvement of Rural and Marginalized Communities

In order to encourage inclusive and sustainable development, the participation of rural and other vulnerable populations is absolutely necessary. People who live in rural areas or in marginalized communities frequently encounter difficulties and obstacles that are specific to them, which makes it more difficult for them to access resources, opportunities, and participate in decision-making processes. In this in-depth study, we will investigate the significance of including these communities in development projects, the difficulties they face, and the tactics and programs that can enable them to have an active role in determining the course of their futures.

1. **The Importance of Participation from Rural and Other Marginalized Communities:**
   Efforts to Reduce Social Disparities:
   In order to eliminate economic and social disparities, one of the most important

first steps is to include underserved and rural populations in the process of development. The gaps in income, living standards, and overall well-being that result from the lack of access to education, healthcare, and economic opportunities that these communities frequently confront are a direct outcome of those factors.

Leveraging the Expertise of the Community:

Communities that are rural or marginalized have rich local knowledge and practices that have been passed down through the generations that can help to sustainable development. By involving them in the decision-making process, you may make use of their experience in fields such as agriculture, resource management, and the preservation of ecosystems.

Providing Community Capacity:

Participation in development programs gives rural and underprivileged groups a sense of ownership over their future, which in turn allows those communities to take control of their own destinies. This empowerment has the potential to lead to increasing levels of self-sufficiency, improved livelihoods, and enhanced levels of communal cohesion.

Making Sure There Is Social Justice:

By addressing the historical and systematic injustices that marginalized communities have endured, inclusive development contributes to the advancement of social justice. It offers a way to make amends for previous disparities and wrongdoings that have occurred.

2. **Obstacles that Stand in the Way of Rural and Marginalized Communities:**

   Limited Opportunities to Receive an Education:

   They are unable to obtain the necessary skills and information because they do not have access to excellent education, which is a problem in many rural and marginalized communities. Because of this education gap, their ability to participate in economic activities and decision-making may be hindered.

   Unequal access to healthcare:

   It is common for marginalized people to have health disparities, which in turn results in greater rates of sickness and a shortened life expectancy. These inequalities are made much worse by a lack of access to information and services regarding healthcare.

   Exclusion from the Economy:

   Communities that are rural or underprivileged frequently face economic exclusion, which can be characterized by a lack of access to financial resources, loans, and markets. This exclusion can contribute to the perpetuation of poverty and therefore inhibit economic growth.

   Stigma and discrimination based on social status:

   These communities can be further marginalized when they are subjected to discrimination and social stigma, which makes it more difficult for them to participate in different elements of society, such as education, work, and participation in local governance.

3. **Initiatives and Strategies for Involving Rural and Other Marginalized Communities:**

Education and Training to Acquire Skills:

Education and training programs are absolutely necessary in order to provide people living in these communities with the information and capabilities they require in order to take an active role in the various areas of development. For the purpose of increasing employability, these programs should place an emphasis on literacy, vocational training, and digital literacy.

Access to Medical Care:

It is essential, in order to improve the health of underserved communities and populations, to broaden access to healthcare services, including preventative care and treatment. The availability of healthcare can be improved through the use of telemedicine, community health workers, and mobile clinics.

Economic Self-Determination:

Individuals in rural and economically disadvantaged communities may be given the ability to participate in economic activities through the implementation of programs such as microfinance, small-scale entrepreneurship, and access to credit. These initiatives must to be modified so that they cater to the particular requirements and assets of the communities involved.

Rights to Use of Land and Resources:

It is of the utmost importance to protect the land and resource rights of rural communities, particularly indigenous groups. Not only do secure land rights safeguard their traditional areas, but they also make it possible to manage resources in a sustainable manner.

The Empowerment of Women :

Involving traditionally excluded populations requires a number of essential components, including gender equality and the empowerment of women. It is necessary for overall development to make provisions to ensure that women have access to education, healthcare, and chances for economic advancement.

4. **Obstacles and Things to Take Into Account:**

Consideration for Other Cultures:

Involving communities that are culturally sensitive and respectful of local customs and traditions is necessary in order to reach rural and marginalized populations. It is important that initiatives for development are congruent with the values and goals of the community.

Goals for Sustaining Sustainable Development:

Providing a formal framework for assessing and achieving development outcomes can be accomplished by aligning community involvement activities with the Sustainable Development Goals (SDGs) outlined by the United Nations.

Construction of Capabilities:

Building up the capabilities of local organizations and community leaders is absolutely necessary in order to ensure the continued success of community participation projects over the long run. Their abilities in management and leadership should be developed through the provision of training and support.

Keeping an eye on things, and giving feedback:

Monitoring and evaluation of community involvement activities on a regular basis are absolutely required in order to assess the efficacy of these programs and make any necessary improvements. This procedure ensures that the programs continue to be useful and relevant to the requirements of the community.

The incorporation of underserved and rural communities into the planning and implementation of development projects is not only an ethical need but also a crucial step toward achieving inclusive and sustainable growth. These cultures are in possession of valuable information, traditions, and skills that have the potential to contribute to holistic development, alleviate disparities, and empower both individuals and communities.

It is vital to address the issues that rural and marginalized groups experience, such as inadequate access to education and healthcare, economic isolation, and social prejudice. Other challenges include healthcare inequities. It is possible to develop a society that is more inclusive and equitable through the implementation of strategies and programs that place an emphasis on economic empowerment, education, healthcare, land and resource rights, and the empowerment of women.

Case examples of successful community engagement programs, such as the Grameen Bank in Bangladesh and Participatory Forest Management in Tanzania, illustrate that such initiatives can lead to major changes in the lives of marginalized groups if they are implemented properly. However, in order to ensure the continued success of these projects over the long term, it is important to give careful consideration to the problems associated with cultural sensitivity, alignment with the SDGs, capacity building, and monitoring and evaluation.

It is not only a goal of development, but also a way to a more just, equitable, and prosperous world in which every individual has the opportunity to succeed and define their own future. Extending the involvement of rural and marginalized groups is not simply a development goal; it is also a path.

4.4 Trading's Role in Reducing Income Inequality

The unequal distribution of income is a prevalent problem on a worldwide scale, and there are enormous wealth and incomes gaps between individuals and communities. Trading plays a crucial role in reducing income disparity because it offers chances for wealth development, income production, and financial inclusion. Although there is no one solution that will work for all instances of this complicated problem, there are several ways that trading may help. During the course of this conversation, we are going to dig into the ways in which trading can help reduce income inequality and the primary processes via which it accomplishes this goal.

1. **Opportunities for Investment Available to Everyone:**
   Increasing Accessibility Through:
   Trading has seen substantial change throughout the course of its history, and as a result, it is now available to a wider variety of people. Access to financial markets has been made more accessible thanks to the proliferation of online trading platforms, smartphone apps, and inexpensive brokerages. Trading activities, including as buying and selling stocks, bonds, and other assets, are open to people from a wide variety of socioeconomic backgrounds. This enables more people to take part in trading activities.
   The Accumulation of Wealth:
   Trading gives individuals the opportunity to amass riches via the investment in various financial assets. When executed with caution, trading has the potential to result in capital appreciation, which, over time, can provide financial gains. Trading allows even people with little resources to participate and benefit from the process, so the growth of wealth is not confined to those who already have a lot of money.

2. **Education and Knowledge Regarding Financial Matters:**
   Knowledge That Can Transform:
   Trading helps people become more financially educated and literate. People who trade frequently educate themselves about the workings of the market, various investing techniques, and various methods of risk management. Because of their level of financial literacy, they are equipped with the knowledge and skills necessary to make educated decisions regarding their investments and improve their overall financial well-being.
   Making Decisions While Having All the Facts:
   Individuals who engage in trading activities are more likely to make well-informed decisions. Traders have an incentive to perform research, examine market patterns, and evaluate risk considerations whenever they make an investment, regardless of whether it's in stocks, bonds, or commodities. The practice of conducting due diligence helps to improve both the investment decisions made and the results obtained financially.

3. **Investment Opportunities That Include Everyone:**
   Investing on a Small Scale:
   Individuals who have few financial means now have more opportunities to invest thanks to the proliferation of micro investing platforms. Individuals are able to invest modest sums of money in a diverse portfolio of assets through the

practice of micro investing. Taking this method reduces the threshold for admission, which in turn makes investment available to a larger pool of people.

Portfolios That Are Diversified:

Individuals are able to construct diversified investment portfolios through the use of trading. Diversification is an essential risk management method that can be used to reduce the likelihood of suffering a loss. Individuals are able to lessen the influence that the volatile market has on their overall wealth by diversifying the asset classes in which they have invested their money.

4. **Obstacles and Things to Take Into Account:**

Instruction on Financial Matters:

Despite the availability of training tools, trading may be a challenging and risky endeavor. It is essential to provide individuals with access to comprehensive financial education and support in order for them to be able to make choices based on accurate information and effectively manage risk.

Behavior That Is Open to Speculation:

Trading can occasionally encourage speculative behavior, which can lead to investments with a high risk and the possibility of financial loss. It is necessary to promote ethical business practices and risk management in order to safeguard individuals from experiencing negative financial outcomes.

Trading has the potential to greatly contribute to reducing income inequality through the democratization of access to investment opportunities, the promotion of financial literacy, and the provision of investment options that are inclusive. It gives people from a wide range of socioeconomic circumstances the ability to amass wealth, make educated decisions regarding their finances, and construct diverse investment portfolios. Case studies of fractional shares and marketplaces that are accessible to cryptocurrencies highlight how innovations in trading have improved financial inclusiveness.

It is essential to prioritize financial education, responsible trading practices, and risk management in order to fully harness the potential of trading in reducing income inequality. This potential can only be realized if income inequality is reduced. Individuals will be able to participate in trade activities with greater self-assurance, which will improve their overall financial well-being and, in the long run, contribute to a more equal distribution of wealth and income.

Chapter 5

Trading and International Trade

Trading and international trade are two aspects of the global economy that are intricately tied to one another and have a substantial impact on one another. Trading, which encompasses a wide variety of financial operations such as buying and selling stocks, commodities, currencies, and other things, is an essential mechanism that plays an important role in the facilitation of international trade. On the other hand, the demand and supply dynamics that drive trading markets are created as a result of international trade, which involves the exchange of commodities and services across international borders. In this all-encompassing research, we will investigate the complex relationship that exists between trading and international trade. More specifically, we will investigate the ways in which financial markets and trading activities impact international trade, as well as the other way around.

1. Comprehending the Nature of International Trade:

Explanation of the Concept and Its Importance:
The buying and selling of products and services between different nations is referred to as international trade. It provides nations with access to resources, markets, and technology that they might not have on their own domestically. As a result, it is a basic engine of economic progress. Specialization is encouraged by international trade, which ultimately results in improved levels of both efficiency and production.

Components that make up international commerce:

1. **Export and Import of Goods:** The process of trading tangible items, such as consumer goods and industrial machinery, with another country.
2. **Trade in Services:** These are transactions that involve services such as tourism, finance, technology, and consulting.
3. **Trade Agreements:** These include both bilateral and multinational pacts that regulate trade ties, tariffs, and market access.

4. **Foreign Direct Investment (FDI):** Investments made by individuals or companies in foreign countries, with the goal of promoting economic cooperation between the two nations.

II. The Importance of Commercial Activity in International Trade:

Rates of Exchange and the Trading of Currencies:

Because it involves the buying and selling of different currencies, trading on foreign exchange (forex) markets is an essential component of international trade. The cost and profitability of foreign transactions are strongly impacted by exchange rates. The prices of currencies are determined by traders and investors in the foreign exchange markets, which, in turn, affect the competitiveness of both exports and imports.

Trading in Commodities and the Role of Global Supply Chains:

In the context of international trade, commodity trading is an extremely important component, notably for the exchange of raw materials and resources. Trading operations can have an effect on the prices of a variety of commodities, including oil, metals, and agricultural items. Commodity traders ensure a continuous flow of these vital goods within global supply chains in order to promote a more efficient economy.

Risk Management, Including Hedging and Mitigation:

There are many potential downsides to engaging in international trade, including swings in currency exchange rates and swings in the prices of various items. Trading instruments such as futures and options give enterprises that participate in international commerce the flexibility to hedge against these risks, which helps maintain price stability and reduces uncertainty.

The Circulation of Capital and Investment:

The movement of capital across international borders, particularly that of foreign direct investment (FDI), is intrinsically related to commercial transactions. When making investment decisions, investors keep an eye on the state of the economy, political stability, and trade policy. These factors all have an impact on the overall investment environment and economic growth.

III. The Influence of International Trade on Commercial Activity:

Volatility in the Market and Potential Investment Opportunities:

Market instability can be triggered by a number of factors related to international commerce, including trade tensions, increases in tariffs, and geopolitical events. Traders keep a close eye on these events in order to locate potential investment opportunities and to mitigate risk.

Performance of the Industry and the Sector:

Different businesses and markets are impacted in unique ways by globalization and international trade. Traders investigate the performance of various markets so they can make educated selections regarding their investments. For instance, trade tariffs may have an effect on the profitability of some businesses, prompting investors to make appropriate adjustments to the portfolios they hold.

Indicators and Data Relating to the Economy:

Data pertaining to international commerce, such as trade balances, export-import figures, and trade policies, are essential economic indicators that traders use to evaluate the state of economies all over the world. The sentiment of the market can be driven by these indications, which can also influence trading decisions.

IV. The Influence of World Events on Commercial Activities and International Trade:

Conflicts Over Trade:

Both domestic and international trade can be significantly impacted by trade wars, such as the one currently raging between the United States and China. Traders pay close attention to talks, changes in tariffs, and retaliatory measures, all of which have the potential to cause market volatility and have an effect on the competitiveness of goods in international markets.

Events of a Geopolitical Nature:

It is possible for international trade and financial markets to be thrown into disarray as a result of geopolitical events such as regional conflicts and political instability. Traders react to these events by making changes to their trading techniques and portfolios in order to mitigate the associated risks.

Shocks to the Economy:

Both international trade and trading markets are impacted when major economic shocks occur, such as the financial crisis that occurred in 2008 or the COVID-19 pandemic. Because of the potential for these events to cause disruptions in supply chains, shifts in consumer behavior, and volatility in the market, traders will need to adjust their strategies to account for the new circumstances.

V. Difficulties and Things to Think About:

Uncertainty Regarding Trade Policy:

Businesses that are involved in international commerce may experience increased levels of uncertainty as a result of frequent shifts in trade policy such as tariffs and trade agreements. Traders are required to keep an eye on these policies and modify their trading methods as needed.

Risks Related to Currency:

Businesses that engage in international trade face significant exposure to risk whenever there is volatility in the exchange rate. Traders and investors employ tactics known as hedging in order to reduce the impact of these risks and guard their own financial interests.

Compliance with Regulations:

Customs procedures, trade sanctions, and trade compliance are all examples of aspects of international trade that are subject to intricate laws. Traders have a responsibility to familiarize themselves with these restrictions in order to conduct their business within the bounds of the law.

Concerns Relating to Ethics and the Environment:

Ethical factors, including labor standards and their influence on the environment, are becoming an increasingly essential aspect of international trade. Traders and investors are supporting ethical and sustainable business practices by including these considerations into their decision-making processes and adopting them into their trading activities.

Trading and international trade are inextricably linked economic activities that both shape and are shaped by one another in the global economy. dealing activities have an effect on international commerce because of currency exchange, commodity dealing, and the reduction of risk; nevertheless, changes in international trade have an effect on trading because they drive market volatility and influence investment decisions. Global events, trade tensions, and economic shocks all have a role in further shaping how these two factors interact with one another.

It is crucial for firms, traders, investors, and policymakers to have a comprehensive understanding of the intricate relationship that exists between trading and international trade. It makes it possible to make judgments that are more informed, improves the ability to manage risks, and gives one the ability to negotiate the fluid and linked terrain of the global economy.

We may work toward more efficient and sustainable international trade by recognizing the diverse character of this relationship. This, in turn, will affect trading markets and contribute to the stability and growth of the global economy.

5.1 Trading's Impact on India's Global Trade

India is one of the most important trading nations since its participation in international trade is essential to the nation's overall economic growth and development. Trading operations, which include exports and imports, are essential to the economic well-being of India. Trade is driven by both sides of the equation. In this in-depth study, we will investigate the complex relationship between trading and India's international trade. More specifically, we will investigate the ways in which trading affects the dynamics of India's exports and imports, as well as the reasons that contribute to the formation of this connection.

1. **A Better Understanding of India's Role in World Trade:**
   The Nature of India's Commercial Scene:
   The practice of exchanging products and services with other nations constitutes India's participation in the global trade system. The landscape of the country's trade has seen tremendous growth in recent decades, with exports and imports encompassing a wide variety of industries, ranging from textiles and manufacturing to information technology and pharmaceuticals. This growth has been accompanied by an increase in the number of countries the country trades with.
   Principal Trading Partners:
   The United States of America, China, the United Arab Emirates, and a number of countries within the European Union are among India's most important

trading partners. These commercial contacts are essential in establishing the scope and nature of India's participation in international trade.

The Composition of Exports and Imports:

The goods that India ships out of the country fall into a wide variety of categories, such as machinery, gems and jewelry, pharmaceuticals, textiles, and agricultural products. Items such as crude oil, electrical goods, machinery, and chemicals are examples of things that can be imported.

2. **The Effects of Trading on India's Participation in Global Trade**

Competition in Export Markets and Currency Exchange Rates:

Trading activity on foreign exchange markets has a direct impact on currency exchange rates, which are a crucial component in India's participation in international trade. The Indian Rupee's decline can help improve the competitiveness of Indian exports, making those goods more appealing to consumers in other countries. The value of the rupee, which in turn affects export dynamics, is determined by traders in the foreign exchange market.

Prices of Commodities and the Cost of Imports:

Trading activity on commodity markets has an effect on the prices of many commodities, especially volatile ones such as crude oil and metals. Because India is a net importer of crude oil, changes in the price of oil can have an effect on the cost of the country's imports. The import cost and trade balance of the nation are both affected by the activities that take place in these marketplaces.

The Commercialization of Agricultural Goods:

India is a leading global exporter of goods from the agricultural sector. India's participation in global trade is inextricably linked to the nation's export and import of agricultural products including rice, wheat, and spices. India's agricultural exports are affected by the fluctuations in the prices of commodities as well as the supply and demand dynamics.

Financial Instruments Available for Commercial Use:

Trading operations in financial markets give methods that can be used to manage risks that are linked with international trade. To protect themselves from the risk of fluctuations in exchange rates, traders utilize financial instruments such as currency futures and options. Both exporters and importers really need to implement this risk management.

3. **Developments in International Trade and Commercial Transactions:**

Alterations to Trade Policy:

Trading decisions and the dynamics of the market are both susceptible to the effects of shifting trade policies, which can include tariffs and trade agreements. Traders pay close attention to the development of these policies so that they may evaluate how they will affect India's participation in global commerce.

Events of a Geopolitical Nature:

The disruption of international trade and the implementation of different trading strategies can be caused by geopolitical events such as regional conflicts and diplomatic tensions. Instability in the political systems of countries with which India does trade can present difficulties for Indian merchants.

4. **Obstacles and Things to Take Into Account:**

Risk Involved With Exchange Rates:

The volatility of exchange rates might provide difficulties for Indian enterprises who are involved in international commerce. The unpredictability that comes with shifts in the value of the currency exchange rate might result in monetary losses. It is essential to implement efficient risk management through the use of trading instruments in order to address these difficulties.

Disruptions in the Supply Chain:

Events on a worldwide scale, such as the COVID-19 pandemic, have the potential to wreak havoc on global supply lines, which in turn could harm India's economy. Traders need to be able to adjust to shifting dynamics of supply and demand and evaluate the impact that disruptions of this kind have on trade operations.

Compliance with Regulations:

Customs processes, trade compliance, and import-export limitations are examples of some of the complicated regulations that are imposed on international trade. In order to conduct business in a manner that is both legal and smooth, merchants are required to traverse the relevant rules.

Trading and India's participation in global trade are intimately interwoven, with trading operations having a substantial impact on the dynamics of the country's export and import commerce. The landscape of India's foreign trade is significantly influenced by a number of critical factors, including fluctuations in exchange rates and commodity prices, the trading of agricultural products, and other key areas. Because traders utilize tools to hedge against currency risks, the importance of financial markets on the management of the risks associated with trade cannot be exaggerated.

In addition, developments in international trade as well as geopolitical events have the potential to disrupt India's trade patterns, which in turn can influence trading strategies and decision-making processes.

Because of the dynamic nature and complexity of the relationship between trading and India's global trade, it is essential for firms, traders, and policymakers in India to maintain vigilance and flexibility.

It is crucial for individuals involved in international trade to have a comprehensive understanding of this complex connection because it enables improved risk management, strategic decision-making, and the capability to traverse the ever-changing landscape of global business. The influence that trading has on India's international commerce highlights the interrelated structure of the global economy as well as the necessity of adopting an all-encompassing strategy for international trade that takes into consideration the complexity of the financial markets.

5.2 Import-Export Dynamics

The dynamics of a nation's imports and exports are fundamental components of its economic activity, and they shape the nation's economic growth, trade relations, and competitiveness on the world stage. The dynamic relationship between a nation's imports (the goods and services that are brought into the country) and its exports (the products and services that are sold to other nations) is one of the most important aspects of the global economy as a whole. This exhaustive study investigates the complexities of import-export dynamics, their relevance in the economy of the entire world, and the factors that influence the interactions that result from these processes.

1. **An Understanding of the Dynamics of Import and Export:**
   Explanation of the Concept and Its Importance:
   The process of importing foreign goods and services into a domestic market is referred to as import dynamics. This allows consumers and businesses to have access to a greater variety of products. The sale of domestic goods and services in international markets, on the other hand, is an example of exporting, and it is one factor that contributes to the expansion of a nation's industrial base and its overall economy.

   Trade Effort and Its Balance:
   The balance of trade is an important indicator that can provide insight into the import-export patterns of a country. A nation has a trade surplus when its exports are higher than its imports; on the other hand, a trade deficit happens when a nation's imports are higher than its exports. When a nation's exports and imports about equal one another, they have what's called a balanced trade situation.

   Relationships with Our Commercial Partners:
   The dynamics of a country's imports and exports are impacted by the trading partners and international relations of that country. Trade flows and the diversity of trading partners are influenced by both bilateral and international trade agreements, as well as trade policies and diplomatic ties with foreign states.

2. **Factors That Influence the Dynamics of Import and Export:**
   Demand from the Market:
   The level of demand in a given market has a significant impact on the dynamics of import and export. The types and amounts of goods and services that are imported and exported are determined by the tastes of consumers as well as the trends that are observed in international markets.

   Advantages in Relation to Others:
   The dynamics of international trade are driven, in large part, by the concept of comparative advantage. Countries tend to specialize in the production of goods and services in areas in which they have a relative advantage or efficiency, and they engage in commerce with other nations to obtain items that they are unable

to produce as efficiently.

The Rates of Exchange:

The dynamics of import and export are substantially impacted by exchange rates. The value of a nation's currency affects both the cost of the nation's imports and the competitiveness of the nation's exports. Changes in currency exchange rates have an effect on trade balances.

Policies Regarding Regulation and Trade:

Import and export patterns can be affected by a nation's trade policies, which may include tariffs, import restrictions, and regulatory frameworks. Imports can be restricted when protectionist measures are implemented, whereas open markets are encouraged by free trade policies.

Global Occurrences and the State of the Economy:

It is possible for the dynamics of imports and exports to be disrupted as a result of international events such as financial crises, pandemics, and geopolitical wars. The state of the economy, be it in a recession or a period of expansion, is another factor that affects the volume of trade.

3. **The Significance of the Dynamics of Import and Export:**

Growth of the Economy:

The dynamics of import and export are important drivers of economic growth. The GDP of a nation can see a boost from exports, while access to essential resources and consumer products can be gained through imports. Maintaining a trading situation that is in balance is beneficial to the economy.

The Development of Industry:

The expansion of domestic industries is mostly driven by exports. The growth of an industry, new job creation, and innovative ideas are all results of increased demand for local products in international markets.

Diversification and Resilience in Practice:

Diversification is encouraged by the dynamics of import and export, which also helps reduce reliance on a single market. The economic resilience of a nation can be strengthened by the practice of diversification in the face of changes in the global economy.

4. **Key Concepts in the Dynamics of Import and Export:**

The Trade Deficit and the Trade Surplus:

When a nation's total exports are higher than its total imports, resulting in a positive balance of trade, the nation is said to have a trade surplus. When exports are less than imports, this results in a negative balance of trade, which is referred to as a trade deficit.

A Look at the Balance of Payments:

The trade balance, which is calculated by subtracting exports from imports, is one component of the balance of payments. Other components include capital and financial movements. It offers an all-encompassing perspective on the monetary dealings that a nation conducts with the rest of the world.

Conditions of Sale:

The ratio of a country's export prices to their import prices is referred to as the terms of trade. When a nation's terms of trade improve, it indicates that it can purchase a greater quantity of imports with the money it earns from selling its goods and services abroad.

5. **Difficulties and Things to Think About:**
Unfair Trade Practices:

The economy can face difficulties if there is a persistent imbalance in trade, such as a substantial deficit in trade. They may result in an increase in external debt, a depreciation of the currency, and the closure of domestic industry.

Tariffs and protectionist policies:

It is possible for protectionist trade policies, such as the introduction of tariffs and other trade barriers, to impede the flow of international trade and have an effect on the dynamics of import and export.

Economic Uncertainty Around the World:

Uncertainty can be introduced into the dynamics of imports and exports as a result of global economic volatility, which can include financial crises and geopolitical tensions. The ever-evolving nature of the market requires that businesses evolve.

Disruptions in the Supply Chain:

It is possible for disruptions in global supply networks, like as those that occurred during the COVID-19 pandemic, to have an effect on the dynamics of import and export by interfering with the movement of products and services.

6. **Projected Developments and Their Implications:**

Electronic commerce and online trade:

The dynamics of international trade are being recast as a result of the expansion of e-commerce and digital trade. Small and medium-sized businesses are able to more easily participate in international trade thanks to the proliferation of online platforms.

Trade that is Both Sustainable and Ethical:

The dynamics of international trade are being affected by a growing consciousness of environmental and social concerns. Global markets are beginning to place a greater emphasis on the implementation of trade practices that are both sustainable and ethical.

The dynamics of import and export are essential to the economic well-being of a nation and to economic connections on a global scale. It is essential for firms, policymakers, and economists to have a solid understanding of the factors that affect these dynamics.

Some examples of these elements are market demand, currency rates, and trade regulations. The crucial role that import-export dynamics play in the world economy is highlighted by the relevance of import-export dynamics in driving economic growth, stimulating industrial expansion, and building economic resilience.

Stakeholders are able to manage the intricacies of global trade difficulties, make decisions that are informed by relevant information, and contribute to a global economy that is more prosperous and integrated when they have an understanding of the complexity of import-export dynamics. The dynamics of import and export are not only about trade; they are also about sculpting the economic landscape of the entire world.

5.3 Role of Trade Agreements and International Partnerships

Trade agreements and international alliances are playing an increasingly important part in determining the character of the landscape of international business in today's increasingly interconnected and interdependent global economy. Trade is facilitated, economic progress is fostered, and inter-nation collaboration is promoted as a result of these agreements, regardless of whether they are bilateral, regional, or multinational. This in-depth investigation investigates the relevance of international trade agreements and partnerships, as well as their influence on the flow of goods around the world and their part in finding solutions to modern problems.

1. **Having an Understanding of International Partnerships and Commercial Agreements:**

The following are the definition and goals:

Trade agreements are legally binding arrangements between two or more countries that specify the terms and circumstances that regulate trade, including tariffs, trade barriers, and market access. Trade agreements can cover a wide range of topics, including tariffs, trade barriers, and market access. The promotion of economic cooperation, the stimulation of trade, and the elimination of impediments to commerce are the primary goals of trade agreements.

Different kinds of trade agreements include:

1. **Agreements Between Two Nations:** Also known as Bilateral Agreements.
2. **Regional Agreements:** These pacts bring together a number of nations from within a particular region.
3. **Multilateral Agreements:** These types of deals involve a number of different countries and are typically organized by international bodies like the World Trade Organization (WTO).

Collaborations with foreign organizations:

The term "international partnerships" refers to greater collaborations between nations on a variety of issues, such as those pertaining to trade, security, and environmental concerns. The scope of international partnerships frequently extends beyond that of trade agreements to include diplomatic, economic, and strategic areas of cooperation.

II. The Importance of International Partnerships and Commercial Agreements:

To Ease Commercial Transactions:

Trade agreements lower or remove trade barriers, such as tariffs and quotas, making it simpler for companies to access international markets and allowing customers to take advantage of a greater variety of goods and services. Trade barriers include tariffs and quotas.

Advancing the Cause of Economic Expansion:

The expansion of market access for goods and services, stimulation of investment, and enhancement of productivity are all outcomes of trade agreements, all of which contribute to economic growth. The subsequent rise in employment possibilities and overall living standards is a direct result of greater economic growth.

Promoting Mutual Understanding and Cooperation:

International relationships, which frequently involve some form of economic cooperation, contribute to the maintenance of political and diplomatic order. These relationships have the potential to help to the maintenance of peace and the resolution of conflicts by fostering conversation and fostering collaboration.

Harmonization of Regulatory Requirements:

It is common practice for trade agreements to contain measures for regulatory harmonization. This helps to ensure that differing technical standards and regulations do not obstruct trade more than is necessary. This may result in enhanced productivity and competitiveness in the marketplace.

III. The following are some of the most important aspects of international partnerships and trade agreements:

The Liberalization of Trade:

The purpose of most trade agreements is to liberalize commerce through the reduction or elimination of tariffs and other types of trade obstacles. This results in an increased flow of goods and services, which in turn creates benefits for all connected parties.

Legal Protection for Intellectual Property:

Protection of intellectual property rights is an essential component of many different types of trade agreements. It protects intellectual property such as patents, copyrights, and trademarks, which in turn fosters innovation and creativity in the global community.

Mechanisms for the Resolution of Disputes:

Trade agreements typically include provisions for settling disagreements between nations that have signed the pact. These processes offer a framework for addressing complaints relating to trade and for implementing the terms of the agreement in a consistent manner.

Access to the Market:

Trade agreements may provide signatory countries with preferential market access. This enables signatory countries to export their goods and services on conditions that are more favorable than those available to non-signatory states.

IV. Trade Accords and International Partnerships in Their Historical Context:

The General Agreement on Tariffs and Trade, also known as GATT, includes the following:

The General Agreement on Tariffs and Trade (GATT) was founded in 1947 and is credited with being the precursor of modern trade accords. The reduction of tariffs and other trade obstacles was one of its primary goals, along with fostering post-war economic recovery and fostering international collaboration.

The World Trade Organization, also known as the "WTO"

The GATT was superseded in 1995 by the World Trade Organization (WTO), which acts as a global forum for the negotiation of trade agreements and the resolution of trade disputes. It comprises a number of agreements that control the commercial exchange of products and services as well as intellectual property.

Agreements Concerning Trade in the Region:

Trade agreements on a regional scale, such as the North American Free Trade Agreement (NAFTA) and the European Union (EU), have been crucial in advancing economic integration and commerce on a regional scale.

V. Impact on International Commerce:

Economic Coalitions of Regional Areas:

The European Union (EU), the Association of Southeast Asian Nations (ASEAN), and Mercosur are examples of regional trade agreements that have resulted in the formation of large economic blocs that impact the patterns and dynamics of global commerce. These regional accords have the ability to radically alter the supply chains and trade flows that operate on a global scale.

Trade Agreements Between Two Countries:

It is common practice to employ bilateral trade agreements to create deeper economic links between two countries. Such agreements also have the ability to increase commerce in particular industries and sectors. They have the potential to open up new doors of opportunity for importers and exporters.

Agreements between Multinational Parties:

In order to develop global trade regulations and to make international trade easier, multilateral agreements such as the World Trade Organization (WTO) are extremely helpful. They provide a venue for addressing issues in international commerce and for creating norms for international trade.

VI. Contemporary Difficulties and Possibilities:

Electronic Commerce and Online Shopping:

The proliferation of digital commerce and online trading brings both new obstacles and opportunities for international trade agreements. In the context of the digital economy, questions about data privacy, cybersecurity, and taxation are becoming an increasingly pressing concern.

Concerns Regarding the Environment and the Climate:

Concerns about the environment and the climate are now being addressed in trade agreements and international partnerships, with an emphasis placed on sustainable and environmentally friendly business operations. These projects have the goal of lowering the impact that international trade has on the environment.

Resilience of the Supply Chain:

In the wake of the COVID-19 epidemic, vulnerabilities in global supply chains came to light. Trade agreements and multinational alliances are currently evaluating various measures to improve the robustness and safety of supply chains.

VII. Difficulties and Things to Take Into Account:

Tensions in International Politics:

Conflicts and tensions on the international political stage can have a negative effect on the efficiency of international trade agreements and partnerships. For example, trade tensions have been caused by disagreements over trade policies between large economies such as the United States and China.

Participation of Stakeholders:

It is essential to take measures to ensure that international trade relationships and agreements are beneficial to all parties involved, including employees, businesses, and the environment. Trade agreements should be crafted in such a way as to prevent some groups from suffering unintended repercussions.

VIII. Prospective Developments and Their Implications:

The rise of digitalization and online shopping:

To accommodate the increasing significance of digital trade and e-commerce, trade agreements

will need to be revised to include provisions for resolving issues relating to data transfers, digital taxation, and consumer protection.

Trade That Is Responsible for the Climate:

Trade agreements will increasingly include provisions for encouraging sustainability and resolving environmental concerns, as well as include provisions for adapting to and mitigating the effects of climate change.

Trade agreements and international alliances are essential tools for molding global commerce, encouraging economic progress, and building an environment conducive to peace and cooperation among nations. These agreements have developed throughout time to address contemporary difficulties such as digital trade, environmental concerns, and the resiliency of supply chains, and they will continue to play a crucial role in the constantly shifting face of international trade. Their importance in fostering prosperity and finding solutions to global difficulties highlights the requirement for ongoing participation and cooperation among states in the world economy.

5.4 Currency Exchange and Forex Trading

The buying and selling of other currencies is an essential part of international business and finance. It entails converting the currency of one nation into the currency of another nation, which makes it possible to conduct business and financial dealings across international borders. Forex trading, which is abbreviated as "forex" and stands for "foreign exchange trading," is the market where currency exchanges take place. We will go into the fundamental ideas behind currency exchange, as well as the workings of foreign exchange trading, as part of this all-encompassing introduction.

1. **Comprehending the Concept of Currency Exchange:**
   Explanation of the Concept and Its Importance:
   Currency exchange, often known as foreign exchange, refers to the process of exchanging the currency of one nation for the currency of another at a rate that has been predetermined. Because it enables participants to conduct business in a variety of currencies, this mechanism plays an essential role in international commerce, travel, and investment.
   The Rates of Exchange:
   The worth of one currency in relation to another is reflected in the market through the use of exchange rates. They are constantly shifting as a result of a variety of factors including interest rates, inflation, the state of the economy, and market sentiment. Depending on the type of currency system that is in use, exchange rates may either be fixed or free to fluctuate.
   The Role of Monetary Policy and Central Banks:
   Through the implementation of various monetary policies, central banks such as the Federal Reserve in the United States or the European Central Bank in the Eurozone have the ability to affect currency exchange rates. Both the value of a currency and its exchange rate can be influenced by actions such as changes in interest rates.
2. **The Fundamentals of Foreign Exchange Trading**

In terms of definition and range:
Trading on the foreign exchange market, often known as FX trading or currency trading, is an activity that takes place on a global scale and consists of participants exchanging one currency for another. Trading foreign currencies, or forex, is done with the primary purpose of making a profit off of varying exchange prices.
Participants in the Foreign Exchange Market:

1. Banks and other financial institutions should participate in large-scale foreign exchange operations.
2. Businesses should hedge the currency risk associated with their foreign activities.
3. **Retail Traders:** Individual investors who participate in the foreign exchange market through online forex brokers.

4. **Speculators:** People who try to make money off of the swings in currency rates.

Significant Currency Pairs:

Trading in foreign exchange typically involves significant currency pairs, such as the Euro and the US Dollar (EUR/USD), the US Dollar and the Japanese Yen (USD/JPY), and the British Pound and the US Dollar (GBP/USD). These pairings have more people trading them, so there is more liquidity available for them.

III. The Workings of Foreign Exchange Trading:

Pairs of Currencies:

Trading in foreign exchange takes place in pairs of currencies, with one currency being purchased while the other being sold. Each currency pair is identified by a base currency, which is the one that is being purchased, and a counter currency, which is the one that is being sold.

Prices to Bid and to Ask for:

The ask price is the lowest amount that a trader is prepared to accept for a currency pair that they are willing to sell, while the bid price is the highest amount that they are willing to pay to purchase that currency pair. The term "spread" refers to the difference in cost between these two offerings.

Use of leverage:

Leverage is a tool that is commonly used in forex trading. Leverage enables traders to handle greater positions with the same amount of capital that they initially invested. Leverage raises the possibility of suffering catastrophic losses, despite the fact that it has the potential to multiply revenues.

Buying and Selling Platforms:

Forex deals are executed through the use of internet trading platforms made available by various brokers. These platforms give users access to real-time price quotations, charts, various tools for technical analysis, as well as the ability to execute orders.

IV. Factors That Have an Effect on Currency Exchange Rates When Trading Forex:

Indicators of the Economy:

Exchange rates are influenced by economic data such as growth rates of GDP and employment figures, as well as inflation rates. When economic performance is strong, currencies tend to appreciate, while when economic performance is weak, currencies tend to depreciate.

Costs of Borrowing:

Interest rate differentials between nations have an effect on currency exchange rates. One nation's higher interest rates attract investment from other nations, which in turn drives up demand for the nation's currency.

Stability on the Political Front:

Currency values can be impacted when there are concerns about political stability or governance. A weakening of the value of a currency may result from political unrest or uncertainty.

Possible Meanings:

Forex traders sometimes engage in speculative trading, in which they forecast future changes in exchange rates based on their study of fundamental and technical elements. Speculative trading can be profitable if done correctly.

V. Risk Management in Foreign Exchange Trading:

Orders to Stop a Loss:

Stop-loss orders are put into place to cut down on the amount of money that could be lost by automatically exiting a trade once it reaches a predetermined price point.

Orders to Take a Profit:

Take-profit orders are orders that are designed to close off a deal whenever a certain amount of a specified profit target has been reached.

Strategies for the Management of Risk:

Forex traders protect their cash and better manage risk by employing a variety of risk management tactics. These strategies include position sizing, diversification, and risk-reward analysis.

VI. Difficulties and Things to Think About:

A High Degree of Volatility:

The foreign exchange (Forex) markets are notorious for their high degree of volatility and their frequent price shifts. Traders need to be able to adjust to constantly shifting market conditions and successfully manage risk.

The Risks of Leverage:

Leverage can significantly enhance profits, but it also significantly raises the risk of suffering substantial losses. Traders who utilize leverage need to do so with caution and should be aware of the hazards involved.

VII. The Importance of Foreign Exchange Trading to the World Economy:

Assisting in the Promotion of International Trade:

By establishing a system through which currency may be converted, foreign exchange trading makes it possible for people and companies to participate in international trade.

Administration of Risk:

Trading foreign currencies provides businesses and investors with the opportunity to hedge against currency risk, so protecting themselves from unfavorable changes in exchange rate.

The Role of Investment and Speculation:

Speculators and investors both have the opportunity to profit from the movement of the currency market when they engage in forex trading. Those who are eager to broaden the scope of their investment portfolios might participate in its financial market.

Currency exchange and foreign exchange trading are important aspects of the global economy because they facilitate international trade, provide a means of risk management, and provide chances for investment. When engaging in foreign exchange trading, the exchange rates that are used are affected by a dynamic interplay of economic, political, and financial elements. Although there are huge potential available in forex trading, there are also inherent hazards that traders need to learn how to manage successfully. Participants can successfully traverse the dynamic and ever-changing world of currency markets if they have a solid understanding of the basics and mechanics of foreign exchange trading.

Chapter 6

Trading Technology and Innovation

Trading software advancements and new ideas have been extremely important factors in the development of the modern financial scene. Trading has seen a tremendous shift over the past several decades, driven by technology improvements that have not only boosted efficiency and accessibility but also introduced new instruments and trading methods. This transformation has been driven by the introduction of new trading strategies and instruments. This investigation of the evolution of trading technology and innovation spans three thousand words and dissects the influence that these developments have had on financial markets, traders, and the economy as a whole.

1. **A Look Back at the Past**

   It is essential to investigate the origins of trade technology and innovation in order to have a proper comprehension of its relevance. Trading has always been an essential component of human civilization, but over the course of history, it has undergone a substantial process of development. In the past, business was performed through face-to-face contacts in real marketplaces. This method severely restricted both the breadth and efficiency of business transactions. During the early stages of commerce, the primary items being traded were goods and commodities; it wasn't until much later that financial instruments such as stocks and bonds were first introduced.

   The first significant advances in trading technology occurred in the 19th century with the introduction of telegraphy and the formation of structured stock exchanges. These two events occurred simultaneously. The trading environment was greatly expanded as a result of this breakthrough since it made it possible for traders to communicate information and execute trades over significant distances. However, this was merely a step in the direction of the fast breakthroughs that have been made in the most recent decades.

2. **Automated Buying and Selling and Electronic Commerce**
   A pivotal turning point in the annals of trading occurred in the latter half of the 20th century with the shift from traditional open outcry trading to modern electronic trading.

   The execution of trades has been both quicker and more efficient because of the development of electronic trading systems, which was made possible by the proliferation of computers and telecommunications networks. This innovation not only sped up the process of trade execution, but it also prepared the way for algorithmic trading, which is decision-making in the financial markets that is carried out by computer programs.

   Trading Based on Algorithms

   The use of instructions that have been pre-programmed in order to carry out trading strategies is at the heart of algorithmic trading, which is also sometimes referred to as "algo trading." The processing of huge volumes of market data in real time by algorithms, the identification of opportunities, and the execution of trades in milliseconds are all possible. Because of this technology, the trading landscape has been completely revolutionized, since it has given traders a competitive edge while also enhancing the liquidity of financial markets. High-frequency trading, or HFT for short, is a subset of algorithmic trading that has grown in prominence in today's markets and has been a source of debate as well as new market developments.

   High-Frequency Trading, abbreviated as "HFT"

   High-frequency trading is characterized by extraordinarily quick execution speeds, with trades occurring in fractions of a second. This type of trading is referred to as "flash trading." HFT companies put a significant amount of money on cutting-edge technology and infrastructure to provide themselves a competitive advantage in terms of speed and efficiency. Although HFT has received acclaim for its role in reducing spreads and providing liquidity, it has also been criticized for the possibility that it exacerbates market volatility and contributes to the instability of market conditions. The discussion over the effect that high-frequency trading has on financial markets is always developing.

3. **Connectivity of Markets and Globalization**
   Not only has the execution of trades been revolutionized by technological advancements, but also the connectivity of global financial markets has been significantly facilitated by these advancements. The proliferation of technologies such as high-speed internet, fiber-optic cables, and data centers has made it far simpler for traders to access and do business in marketplaces located all over the world. As a direct consequence of this, the world's financial markets have become more interdependent and integrated.

   Connectivity of the Market

   Traders are now able to access a diverse range of financial products from any location in the world thanks to the proliferation of electronic trading platforms and networks. This level of market connectedness has enabled traders to take advantage of new opportunities, including the ability to diversify their holdings and react in real time to happenings around the world.

The phenomenon of globalization

Trading technology has been a significant enabler of the globalization of financial markets in recent years. Now that traders and investors can interact with worldwide markets, there has been an increase in the movement of capital across borders. Because of this globalization, regulators and market participants face new problems, as it calls for a more coordinated and harmonized approach to market oversight and risk management.

4. **Financial Technology and Other Innovative Disruptors**

FinTech refers to the intersection of finance and technology, which has resulted in a surge of innovative trading practices that have the potential to significantly disrupt existing markets. FinTech startups and established financial institutions are both leveraging technology to develop novel solutions that challenge existing trading methods and democratize access to financial markets. These solutions are being created with the goal of disrupting traditional trading patterns.

Brokerages available online

Trading has become more accessible to more people as a result of the rise of online brokerages. They make it easier for individuals to start trading by providing user-friendly platforms, lower trading fees, and access to a large selection of financial goods. This makes it possible for individuals to start trading more easily. This trend has been exacerbated even more by the proliferation of commission-free trading apps.

The Technology Behind Cryptocurrencies and Blockchain

Traditional finance has been shaken up by the proliferation of cryptocurrencies and the technology behind blockchains. Trading and settlement procedures are expected to benefit from increased security, transparency, and efficiency thanks to blockchain's decentralized ledger technology. In addition, cryptocurrencies like Bitcoin have given rise to a new asset class, which has resulted in the creation of new chances for trading.

Trading through crowdsourcing platforms and social trading

The use of crowdsourcing in trading and the development of social trading platforms are becoming increasingly common. Traders are able to discuss their trading techniques and transactions with a community of investors by using these platforms. Traders new to the market might pick up useful information from more seasoned market participants, while more seasoned traders can make money off of their expertise and attract new customers.

The rise of the robot advisors

Robo-advisors are software programs that give automated, low-cost investing advice and management of portfolios.

These programs make use of algorithms. These platforms have gained popularity as a result of their capacity to offer retail investors portfolios that are diversified, risk-adjusted, and risk-managed, hence lowering the demand for traditional financial advisors.

5. **Regulation and Risk Management**

As a result of the rapid development of trading technology, regulatory actions have become necessary in order to maintain the integrity of the market, maintain fairness, and safeguard investors. Global regulators have been hard at work to find a middle ground that allows them to encourage innovation while also reducing the dangers that are connected with trading systems that are becoming increasingly complicated.

Problems Associated with Regulations

The world of trading technology moves at a breakneck speed, and it can be difficult for regulators to keep up with it. In the process of tackling problems such as market manipulation, insider trading, and systemic risk, they have the responsibility of ensuring that market participants adhere to fair and ethical norms.

Cybersecurity Measures, and Efforts to Reduce Risk

The probability of cyberattacks and system breakdowns also rises in tandem with the development of trading technologies. Participants in the market are obligated to apply stringent cybersecurity measures and build contingency plans in order to lessen the impact of any technological failures they may have.

Monitoring of the Market

The authorities in charge of market regulation have made significant investments in cutting-edge surveillance equipment in order to track market activity and identify anomalies. These surveillance systems use data analytics and machine learning to identify possible market abuses such as spoofing, layering, and insider trading in order to prevent these types of illegal activities.

6. **Artificial intelligence and machine learning**

The fields of artificial intelligence (AI) and machine learning are quickly becoming important components of trading technology. These technologies are put to use for an extremely diverse variety of purposes, ranging from predictive analytics to the construction of trading strategies. Artificial intelligence (AI) and machine learning have the potential to revolutionize trading by analyzing massive amounts of data and detecting patterns that are beyond the capability of human traders. Consequently, AI and machine learning have the potential to transform trading.

Analytics Predictive of the Future

Utilizing both historical and real-time data, predictive analytics attempts to estimate the behavior of future market movements. Trading signals can be generated by machine learning algorithms, which can then be used to assist traders in making more educated decisions by analyzing a wide variety of variables and data sources.

Processing of natural language (also known as NLP)

The news, social media, and other textual data sources are analyzed with natural language processing so that market sentiment may be determined, and probable price changes caused by news can be forecasted. Algorithms that use natural language processing (NLP) can quickly evaluate and classify huge volumes of information, allowing them to discover pertinent market trends and news events.

Interpretation of Feelings

In order to evaluate the total sentiment of market players, artificial intelligence and machine learning are combined in sentiment analysis. Traders can acquire insights into market mood by examining market commentary found in news stories, social media posts, and news articles, which in turn helps them forecast market swings.

7. **Data on the Market and Large Amounts of Data**

The financial markets have entered the era of big data thanks to the advent of trading technology. Opportunities for traders and investors to get a more profound understanding of the dynamics of the market and to make decisions that are more informed are created by the sheer volume and variety of data that is generated by electronic trading systems.

Data Sources for the Market

The generation of a large amount of data by electronic trading platforms includes order flow,

trade executions, price quotes, and other market-related information. Traders that are interested in developing trading methods based on real-time as well as historical market data will find this data to be of tremendous value.

Examination of the Data

For the purpose of gleaning useful insights from large amounts of data, sophisticated data analysis methods such as data mining and machine learning are utilized. Traders can utilize these insights to improve their trading methods and make risk management decisions that are more informed.

Different Kinds of Data

For the purpose of gaining an informational advantage in trading, one can benefit from utilizing alternative data, which refers to the utilization of non-traditional data sources such as satellite imagery, credit card transactions, and weather data. Alternative data have the potential to offer fresh perspectives on a variety of business sectors and consumer marketplaces.

8. **The Prospects for Business Innovation and Technology in the Future**

There are no indications that the progression of trading technology will ever slow down. The future of financial markets and trading practices is likely to be influenced in significant ways by a number of developing trends and technology.

Computing on the Quantum Level

Trading could undergo a fundamental shift as a result of the revolutionary potential of quantum computing, which can handle enormous volumes of data at breakneck speeds. Classical computers are unable to solve the difficult mathematical problems and run the complicated simulations that quantum computers are able to do.

(DeFi) stands for "decentralized finance"

Decentralized finance, also known as DeFi (acronym for "decentralized finance"), is an ecosystem of blockchain-based financial goods and services that aims to mimic traditional financial services without the involvement of middlemen. By providing decentralized lending, borrowing, trading, and other financial services, DeFi platforms are giving traditional financial institutions a run for their money.

Digital currencies issued by central banks are known as CBDCs

Bank of the nation The use of digital currencies as a digital substitute to physical cash is now being investigated by a number of central banks. CBDCs have the potential to revolutionize payment systems and settlement procedures, which will in turn have an effect on the functioning of financial markets.

Investing with a Focus on Environmental, Social, and Governance (ESG)

Considerations pertaining to ESG are being introduced into trading methods more and more. Traders are incorporating environmental, social, and governance (ESG) factors into their investing decisions by employing technology to examine data linked to ESG, evaluate the sustainability policies of companies, and more.

The combined use of Augmented and Virtual Reality

Research is being conducted into the use of augmented and virtual reality technology for training and simulation purposes in the trading industry. Traders can utilize these technologies to improve their decision-making and risk management by visualizing market data and trading situations.

From the early days of face-to-face trading in physical marketplaces to the present day, when high-speed electronic trading, AI-powered algorithms, and big data analysis are the norm, there has been a significant advancement in both trading technology and innovation. There is no denying the significance of these technical breakthroughs, which have led to an increase in the market's complexity, accessibility, and efficiency.

When we consider the years to come, it is certain that the technology used in trading will continue to advance. Emerging developments that will have an effect on the financial markets include, but are not limited to, quantum computing, decentralized finance, CBDCs, ethically responsible investing, and augmented and virtual reality. However, with innovation comes a host of obstacles, including as regulatory worries, the potential for breaches in cybersecurity, and the requirement that traders and other market players engage in continual education and adapt.

It is essential for traders, investors, regulators, and technologists to remain informed, communicate with one another, and adapt to the rapidly evolving world of trading technology and innovation in this environment, which is characterized by constant change. Trading will continue to evolve, and as it does, it will have an impact that is increasingly deep on the economy and society as a whole. Because of this, it will be an important topic to study and investigate for many years to come.

6.1 Technological Advancements in Trading

Because of the rapid improvements in technology that have taken place in recent decades, the trading industry has gone through a period of profound change. These changes have been brought about by the revolution that has taken place in the financial sector. Trading has not only become more accessible and efficient as a result of the incorporation of cutting-edge technology, but it has also given rise to the development of new trading instruments and methods. The key technological developments in trading are discussed in this article, along with the impact that these advancements have had on the financial markets.

1. **Venues for Transactions Conducted Online**

   An important turning point in the annals of trading history is the use of electronic trading platforms as an alternative to the more conventional open outcry trading. The buying and selling of securities and other financial instruments has been fundamentally altered as a result of the proliferation of electronic trading platforms. Traders are given the ability to electronically execute orders through the use of these platforms, which results in a trading method that is both quicker and more effective.

   Swiftness: The use of electronic trading eliminates the time lags that are associated with more conventional methods, making it possible for orders to be executed almost instantly.

   Accessibility: Traders are able to access electronic trading platforms from anywhere in the world as long as they have an internet connection. This removes the requirement that traders be physically present.

   Real-time data and information about the market are easily accessible, which increases transparency for both traders and investors.

   Cost Savings Because there is no need for middlemen when engaging in electronic trading, the associated transaction fees are often lower than those associated with traditional trading.

   Automatization: The use of electronic trading platforms can help to facilitate algorithmic trading, which in turn enables the automated execution of trading methods.

2. **Trading Based on Algorithms**

   In the realm of finance, the implementation of algorithmic trading, also referred to as algo trading, represents a huge step forward in terms of technological development. Utilizing computer algorithms to carry out trading techniques in an automated fashion is involved in this approach. Because it can evaluate enormous amounts of data and arrive to trading conclusions in a fraction of a second, algorithmic trading has become increasingly common in the world's financial markets.

Trading Algorithms Trading algorithms are developed to follow particular trading methods such as trend-following, arbitrage, and market making.

Data Analysis Trading signals are generated by algorithms after they conduct an analysis of market data, such as price fluctuations and information on order books.

Execution: Algorithms carry out trades based on the criteria and trading signals that have been

specified, typically with very little involvement from a human trader.

Risk Management: Algorithms used in risk management help to control the exposure that trading positions have to risk and lower the likelihood that big losses will occur.

The greater liquidity and improved efficiency of trading that algorithmic trading has brought forth can be attributed to this trend. Additionally, it has made way for high-frequency trading, commonly known as HFT, which is a subcategory of algorithmic trading.

3. **High-Frequency Trading (HFT)**

   Ultra-Fast Execution: High Frequency Trading (HFT) tactics try to execute trades in fractions of a second, capitalizing on inefficiencies in the market and price differences.

   Co-Location High-frequency trading companies typically position their trading servers in close proximity to the data centers of exchanges in order to reduce the impact of latency.

   Scalability refers to the ability of high-frequency trading (HFT) systems to manage enormous volumes of trades, which might involve thousands of orders per second.

   Both supporters and opponents of HFT have voiced their opinions. The argument made in favor of it is that it reduces spreads and increases liquidity in the markets, both of which are ultimately beneficial to all players. On the other side, detractors are concerned about the possibility of market instability and the unfair advantages that HFT companies might have.

4. **Connectivity of Markets and Globalization**

   Trading technology has markedly improved market connectivity and contributed greatly to the globalization of financial markets. The proliferation of technologies such as high-speed internet, fiber-optic cables, and data centers has made it far simpler for traders to access and do business in marketplaces located all over the world. As a direct consequence of this, the world's financial markets have become more interdependent and integrated.

Connectivity of the Market

Traders are now able to access a diverse range of financial products from any location in the world thanks to the proliferation of electronic trading platforms and networks. This level of market connectedness has enabled traders to take advantage of new opportunities, including the ability to diversify their holdings and react in real time to happenings around the world.

The phenomenon of globalization

Trading technology has been a significant enabler of the globalization of financial markets in recent years. Now that traders and investors can interact with worldwide markets, there has been an increase in the movement of capital across borders. Because of this globalization, regulators and market participants face new problems, as it calls for a more coordinated and harmonized approach to market oversight and risk management.

5. ## Management of Risk and Regulatory Compliance

As a result of the rapid development of trading technology, regulatory actions have become necessary in order to maintain the integrity of the market, maintain fairness, and safeguard investors. Global regulators have been hard at work to find a middle ground that allows them to encourage innovation while also reducing the dangers that are connected with trading systems that are becoming increasingly complicated.

Problems Associated with Regulations

The world of trading technology moves at a breakneck speed, and it can be difficult for regulators to keep up with it. In the process of tackling problems such as market manipulation, insider trading, and systemic risk, they have the responsibility of ensuring that market participants adhere to fair and ethical norms.

Protection against cyberattacks

The probability of cyberattacks and system breakdowns also rises in tandem with the development of trading technologies. Participants in the market are obligated to apply stringent cybersecurity measures and build contingency plans in order to lessen the impact of any technological failures they may have.

Monitoring of the Market

The authorities in charge of market regulation have made significant investments in cutting-edge surveillance equipment in order to track market activity and identify anomalies. These surveillance systems use data analytics and machine learning to identify possible market abuses such as spoofing, layering, and insider trading in order to prevent these types of illegal activities.

6. ## Artificial intelligence and machine learning

The fields of artificial intelligence (AI) and machine learning are quickly becoming important components of trading technology. These technologies are put to use for an extremely diverse variety of purposes, ranging from predictive analytics to the construction of trading strategies. Artificial intelligence (AI) and machine learning have the potential to revolutionize trading by analyzing massive amounts of data and detecting patterns that are beyond the capability of human traders. Consequently, AI and machine learning have the potential to transform trading.

Analytics Predictive of the Future

Utilizing both historical and real-time data, predictive analytics attempts to estimate the behavior of future market movements. Trading signals can be generated by machine learning algorithms, which can then be used to assist traders in making more educated decisions by analyzing a wide variety of variables and data sources.

Processing of natural language (also known as NLP)

The news, social media, and other textual data sources are analyzed with natural language processing so that market sentiment may be determined, and probable price changes caused by news can be forecasted. Algorithms that use natural language processing (NLP) can quickly evaluate and classify huge volumes of information, allowing them to discover pertinent market trends and news events.

Interpretation of Feelings

In order to evaluate the total sentiment of market players, artificial intelligence and machine learning are combined in sentiment analysis. Traders can acquire insights into market mood by examining market commentary found in news stories, social media posts, and news articles, which in turn helps them forecast market swings.

7. **Data on the Market and Large Amounts of Data**

The financial markets have entered the era of big data thanks to the advent of trading technology. Opportunities for traders and investors to get a more profound understanding of the dynamics of the market and to make decisions that are more informed are created by the sheer volume and variety of data that is generated by electronic trading systems.

Data Sources for the Market

The generation of a large amount of data by electronic trading platforms includes order flow, trade executions, price quotes, and other market-related information. Traders that are interested in developing trading methods based on real-time as well as historical market data will find this data to be of tremendous value.

Examination of the Data

For the purpose of gleaning useful insights from large amounts of data, sophisticated data analysis methods such as data mining and machine learning are utilized. Traders can utilize these insights to improve their trading methods and make risk management decisions that are more informed.

Different Kinds of Data

For the purpose of gaining an informational advantage in trading, one can benefit from utilizing alternative data, which refers to the utilization of non-traditional data sources such as satellite imagery, credit card transactions, and weather data. Alternative data have the potential to offer fresh perspectives on a variety of business sectors and consumer marketplaces.

8. The Prospects for Financial Market Technology

There is still a long way to go until the development of trading technology is complete. The future of financial markets and trading practices is likely to be influenced in significant ways by a number of developing trends and technology.

Computing on the Quantum Level

Trading could undergo a fundamental shift as a result of the revolutionary potential of quantum computing, which can handle enormous volumes of data at breakneck speeds. Classical computers are unable to solve the difficult mathematical problems and run the complicated simulations that quantum computers are able to do.

(DeFi) stands for "decentralized finance"

Decentralized finance, also known as DeFi (acronym for "decentralized finance"), is an ecosystem of blockchain-based financial goods and services that aims to mimic traditional financial services without the involvement of middlemen. By providing decentralized lending, borrowing, trading, and other financial services, DeFi platforms are giving traditional financial institutions a run for their money.

Digital currencies issued by central banks are known as CBDCs

Bank of the nation The use of digital currencies as a digital substitute to physical cash is now being investigated by a number of central banks. CBDCs have the potential to revolutionize payment systems and settlement procedures, which will in turn have an effect on the functioning of financial markets.

Investing with a Focus on Environmental, Social, and Governance (ESG)

Considerations pertaining to ESG are being introduced into trading methods more and more.

Traders are incorporating environmental, social, and governance (ESG) factors into their investing decisions by employing technology to examine data linked to ESG, evaluate the sustainability policies of companies, and more.

The combined use of Augmented and Virtual Reality

Research is being conducted into the use of augmented and virtual reality technology for training and simulation purposes in the trading industry. Traders can utilize these technologies to improve their decision-making and risk management by visualizing market data and trading situations.

6.2 Algorithmic Trading and High-Frequency Trading

Trading using algorithms and high-frequency trading (also known as HFT) are two cutting-edge trading tactics that are closely related to one another and have had a substantial impact on the evolution of the financial markets. In order to carry out transactions quickly and effectively, these technologies rely on computer algorithms and high-speed data processing. In this piece, we will go into the ideas of algorithmic trading and high-frequency trading (HFT), investigating their complexities along with their benefits and potential drawbacks.

1. **Trading Based on Algorithms**
   Trading Strategies: Algorithmic trading has the ability to perform a diverse range of trading strategies, including trend-following, statistical arbitrage, market creation, and many others. The goals of the trader and the amount of risk they are willing to take influence the approach they choose.
   Analysis of Market Data Trading signals are generated by algorithms after they process massive volumes of market data such as price quotes, information from order books, and news feeds. The timing of purchases and sales of securities is determined by these signals.
   Algorithmic trading relies heavily on automation, which is a key component of automation. After being built, an algorithm is able to carry out trades around the clock and respond immediately to changes in the state of the market.
   Risk Management Algorithms for risk management are incorporated into trading strategies in order to exercise control over position sizes and reduce the likelihood of incurring losses.
   Efficiency: Algorithmic trading is extremely efficient, since it executes orders at the best possible prices and reduces the impact on the market to a minimum. The significance of this cannot be overstated for huge institutional investors.
   The following are some advantages of algorithmic trading:
   Speed: Algorithms are able to execute deals far more quickly than human traders, allowing them to capitalize on opportunities that are only available for a limited time.
   Accuracy: In order to maintain trading discipline, algorithms always adhere to the pre-defined rules and do so devoid of any emotional biases.
   Diversification is made possible by the fact that algorithmic trading strategies can be applied to a wide variety of different financial instruments and markets.
   Reduced Expenditures: Lower trading costs are the outcome of reduced human intervention and the capability to seize advantageous price opportunities.
   Market makers supply liquidity through algorithmic trading by quoting buy and sell orders, which helps to bring the bid-ask spread closer together.

2. **High-Frequency Trading (also known as HFT)**
   Ultra-Fast Execution: High Frequency Trading (HFT) tactics try to execute trades in fractions of a second, capitalizing on inefficiencies in the market and price differences.
   Processing of Market Data: High-frequency trading businesses use complex algorithms to process and analyze massive volumes of market data in order to

locate arbitrage possibilities, price differences, and order flow patterns.

Scalability refers to the ability of high-frequency trading (HFT) systems to manage enormous volumes of trades, which might involve thousands of orders per second.

The following is a list of advantages to high-frequency trading:

Market Liquidity High-Frequency Trading (HFT) supplies the markets with liquidity by continuously quoting buy and sell orders. This helps to reduce bid-ask spreads and improves market efficiency.

Price Discovery High-Frequency Trading (HFT) is beneficial in that it expediently assists in the discovery of accurate market prices that are reflective of the most recent information and trading activity.

Narrow Spreads As a result of the competition among HFT businesses, spreads have been narrower, which has made trading more cost-effective for other market participants.

Arbitrage Opportunities High-frequency trading is able to recognize and capitalize on price differences across a variety of marketplaces and exchanges, which helps to make markets more efficient.

Risk Mitigation High-Frequency Trading's ability to quickly react to unfavorable market conditions can help mitigate the possibility of suffering significant financial losses.

Nevertheless, it is necessary to point out that HFT has been the subject of criticism and worries:

Critics assert that high-frequency trading (HFT) can exacerbatingly increase market volatility, which can result in abrupt and significant price shifts.

Market Manipulation There are worries over the potential for high-frequency trading (HFT) to engage in manipulative trading tactics like as spoofing and layering. These actions are examples of market manipulation.

Unfair Advantage It's possible that high-frequency trading companies have an unfair advantage over traditional traders because they have access to the most cutting-edge technology and data streams.

Systemic Risk: The rapidity and complexity of high-frequency trading (HFT) systems may add to systemic risk, as was seen in the "Flash Crash" in 2010.

Examination by Regulators High-frequency trading (HFT) has captured the attention of regulators, which has resulted in enhanced monitoring and the development of regulations to minimize potential abuses.

3. **How High-Frequency Trading and Algorithmic Trading Intersect with One Another**

Both high-frequency trading and algorithmic trading are inextricably linked to one another. The execution of high-frequency trading (HFT) methods frequently depends on algorithmic procedures. Both algorithmic trading and high-frequency trading make use of computer algorithms to automate trading choices; hence, it can be difficult to differentiate between the two in this setting. For instance, high-frequency trading (HFT) companies frequently use market-making tactics, which entail continuously quoting buy and sell orders and modifying prices based on the conditions of the market. In the same way that algorithmic trading does, these techniques need to use algorithms that can react quickly to shifting levels of supply and demand. However, the primary difference resides in the speed of execution, with the goal of high-frequency trading (HFT) techniques being to complete transactions more quickly than those of typical algorithmic trading strategies.

In addition, algorithmic trading can involve a wider variety of techniques, including investment strategies with a longer time horizon, whereas high-frequency trading (HFT) is largely focused on ultra-fast trading operations with short time horizons.

4. **Regulatory Oversight and Safety Measures**

The rapid development of high-frequency trading and algorithmic trading has made regulatory actions necessary in order to defend the integrity of the market, maintain fairness, and safeguard investors. Global regulators have been hard at work to find a middle ground that allows them to encourage innovation while also reducing the dangers that are connected with trading systems that are becoming increasingly complicated.

The world of algorithmic trading and high-frequency trading (HFT) moves at a breakneck speed, making it difficult for regulators to keep up with the industry. In addition to tackling concerns such as market manipulation, insider trading, and systemic risk, they have the responsibility of ensuring that market participants adhere to fair and ethical principles.

Risk Management: Both algorithmic trading and high-frequency trading require stringent risk management processes in order to control the exposure of trading positions and cut down on the possibility of suffering big losses. The algorithms that are used in risk management are developed to react to unfavorable market situations and to stop catastrophic losses.

Market Surveillance: In order to monitor market activity and identify abnormalities, regulatory authorities have made substantial investments in very sophisticated surveillance systems. These surveillance systems use data analytics and machine learning to identify possible market abuses such as spoofing, layering, and insider trading in order to prevent these types of illegal activities.

Interventions by Regulatory agencies: In response to the issues raised by algorithmic trading and high-frequency trading (HFT), regulatory agencies have enacted particular regulations. Circuit breakers, minimum resting intervals for orders, and trading halts in the event of significant price swings are some examples of the regulations that may be included in this category.

6.3 Blockchain and Cryptocurrencies

A decentralized and secure framework for transactions and data storage has been introduced thanks to the advent of blockchain technology and cryptocurrencies, which have changed the modern financial environment. The idea of blockchain, which is a distributed ledger system, is at the heart of this technical innovation. Blockchain is the technology that ensures the smooth operation of cryptocurrencies such as Bitcoin, Ethereum, and a plethora of other digital currencies. Together, these technological advancements have fundamentally altered how we think about and interact with digital assets and transactions, ushering in a brand-new era in which individuals have greater control over their financial situations and more access to information.

In its most basic form, blockchain can be seen as a decentralized and unchangeable ledger that keeps track of transactions over a network of several computers. As a result of each transaction, which is referred to as a block, being linked to the one before it, a chain of blocks is created, hence the name "blockchain." Any attempt to modify a single block would need the modification of all following blocks, which would make the operation nearly difficult. As a result, this structure assures that the full transaction history is open to the public and cannot be altered in any way. This quality offers a comprehensive security foundation, which has gained extensive interest from a variety of different industries.

One of the most important advancements that has taken place in recent times is the incorporation of cryptocurrency into the ecosystem of blockchain technology. This new financial paradigm is being led by Bitcoin, the world's first decentralized digital currency, which has emerged as the paradigm's flag bearer. Because Bitcoin transactions are validated by network nodes using cryptography, it is resistant to fraudulent activities and ensures safe peer-to-peer transactions. Because Bitcoin operates without the need for a central authority, it is resistant to fraudulent operations. Ethereum, another well-known cryptocurrency, is responsible for popularizing the idea of smart contracts, which remove the need for third parties in the implementation of programmed agreements.

The proliferation of cryptocurrencies has given rise to discussions regarding the possible effects that they may have on economies all over the world, regulatory frameworks, and the future of finance. Cryptocurrencies, according to its proponents, have the potential to democratize financial institutions by making it possible for unbanked and underbanked populations to get access to banking services. This, in turn, would foster financial inclusion and empowerment. Additionally, the openness and safety provided by blockchain technology has the potential to increase trust in financial transactions, thereby lowering the risk of fraudulent activities and cutting down on the expenses of operations connected with intermediaries.

However, the growth of cryptocurrencies has also prompted worries surrounding regulatory control, market volatility, and the potential misuse for criminal activities like as money laundering and tax evasion. These concerns have been brought about as a result of the proliferation of cryptocurrencies. The necessity to find a balance between supporting innovation and safeguarding investors from the potential hazards connected with the volatility nature of cryptocurrency markets is a challenge that regulatory agencies all over the world are currently attempting to solve. Additionally, the environmental impact of cryptocurrency mining, particularly in the case of energy-intensive proof-of-work consensus algorithms, has spurred arguments about sustainability and the requirement for more eco-friendly alternatives. This is because these algorithms are required to validate transactions using a large amount of energy.

In spite of these obstacles, the blockchain technology that underpins cryptocurrencies is continuing to attract interest in other contexts. It has the potential to be applied in a variety of fields, such as healthcare, voting systems, identity verification, and supply chain management. The decentralized and transparent nature of blockchain has the potential to enhance efficiency, security, and accountability, thereby addressing concerns that have persisted for a long time relating to data privacy and trust in digital transactions.

It is vital for stakeholders to collaborate and build robust regulatory frameworks that stimulate innovation while maintaining consumer safety as the globe continues to explore the possibilities afforded by blockchain technology and cryptocurrencies. It is highly possible that the development of this technology will transform established financial structures, so opening up new doors to economic empowerment, transparency, and efficiency in the marketplace on a worldwide scale.

6.4 The Future of Trading Technology in India

The combination of digital innovation, regulatory developments, and changing investor preferences is going to create a huge transition in the future of trading technology in India, and this transformation is certain to have a significant impact. The Indian trading environment is undergoing a fundamental change toward online and mobile trading platforms as a result of the fast digitization of financial services, the increasing adoption of smartphones, and the increasing availability of high-speed internet connectivity. This move has the potential to democratize access to financial markets and allow a larger segment of the public to participate in trading and investing activities. This shift has the ability to democratize access to financial markets and empower a larger segment of the population.

Adoption of advanced trading platforms and tools that give real-time market data, analytical insights, and configurable trading strategies is one of the important trends that will shape the future of trading technology in India. This adoption is one of the key trends influencing the future of trading technology in India. It is anticipated that there will be an increase in demand for user-friendly interfaces, comprehensive risk management tools, and algorithmic trading capabilities as investors attempt to increase the level of control and transparency they exercise in their trading activities. In addition, the incorporation of artificial intelligence and machine learning algorithms into trading platforms is poised to transform market analysis, decision-making, and risk assessment, thereby providing investors with the ability to make investment decisions based on facts.

In addition, the growth of the fintech ecosystem in India is making it easier for creative trading solutions to be developed. These solutions are designed to meet the needs of many types of investors, such as individual traders, institutional traders, and wealth management companies. Robo-advisory services, automated portfolio management, and social trading platforms are gaining popularity among investors because they offer investors personalized investment advice, tactics for portfolio diversification, and opportunities for collaborative trading. The dynamics of the Indian trade landscape are likely to be reshaped as a result of this development, which will create a culture of informed decision-making and diversified investment portfolios.

The integration of cryptocurrency trading platforms in India should become much simpler as a result of recent regulatory changes and technological developments, which are helping to pave the way for this. The Indian trading market is witnessing a boom in demand for secure and regulated cryptocurrency exchanges as a result of the growing global adoption of digital assets. This provides investors with the opportunity to diversify their portfolios and explore other investment possibilities. As the legislative framework for cryptocurrencies continues to undergo change, it is anticipated that the future of trading technology in India will see a deeper integration of digital assets inside the mainstream financial ecosystem. This will produce new opportunities for investors and help to broaden access to financial services.

Chapter 7

Challenges and Risks in Trading

Trading on financial markets has the potential to be successful, but it is not without its share of difficulties and risks. Traders that are successful comprehend these dangers and successfully mitigate their effects. In the course of this all-encompassing investigation, we are going to look into the myriad of difficulties and dangers that traders face. In this lesson, we will discuss not just the actual market dangers but also the psychological obstacles that traders encounter, as well as the methods and instruments that may be used to manage those risks.

Risks in the Market:

Volatility of the Market:

The financial markets are characterized by their inherent tendency for volatility, sometimes known as price fluctuations. It's possible for traders to make huge profits or loses as a result of this. Rapid market movement can be triggered by a variety of factors, including economic and political developments as well as unexpected news. Traders are need to adjust their practices to account for these shifts and use risk management methods.

Risks Related to Liquidity:

The presence of liquidity risk occurs when a market does not have sufficient participants or trading volume, which makes it difficult to execute trades at the prices that are intended. This presents a unique set of challenges for traders who deal with illiquid assets or who trade huge amounts. Slippage is a potential outcome of liquidity risk, which describes a situation in which the executed price is different from the anticipated price.

Risk posed by a Counterparty:

Counterparty risk, which is also known as default risk, is the danger that one of the parties involved in a trade may fail to live up to their end of the bargain and fulfill their responsibilities. It is common in over-the-counter (OTC) markets, but it can be reduced by utilizing reliable counterparties and clearinghouses. Traders stand to lose money in the event that their broker goes bankrupt.

Risk to the System:

A financial market's exposure to systemic risk is the danger that the market will fail owing to widespread problems that affect the whole financial system as a whole. A worldwide economic catastrophe is one of the potential triggers that could set this in motion. Traders can reduce their exposure to systemic risk by diversifying their holdings and keeping themselves updated about macroeconomic conditions.

Problems of a Psychological Nature:

Decisions Influenced by Emotions:

The judgment of a trader can be clouded by emotions like fear and greed, which can lead to the trader making rash choices. A common outcome of making decisions based on emotions is engaging in excessive trading, engaging in revenge trading, or neglecting the rules of risk management. In order to steer clear of these traps, traders need to cultivate emotional control.

Fear of taking a loss:

A significant number of traders are driven more by their desire to avoid losses than by the possibility of making profits. This might cause a person to cling on to losing positions for too long in the hope that they will turn around, or it can cause them to exit winning ones too soon. Trading must be approached in a manner that is rational and methodical in order to get past the fear of loss.

The phenomenon known as confirmation bias:

Traders frequently look for information and research that supports the beliefs or positions they already hold in the market. A lack of objectivity and the inability to examine alternate points of view can result when traders are influenced by their prejudice. Traders should aggressively seek out information from a variety of sources in order to reduce the impact of confirmation bias.

A lack of humility:

Traders who are overconfident may be more likely to disregard warning flags and take unnecessary risks. Even for the most seasoned specialists, dealing in financial markets is fraught with risk, thus it is critical to keep a humble attitude and be aware of this reality.

Strategies for the Mitigation of Risk:

Administration of Risk:

The use of effective risk management measures, including as establishing stop-loss orders, position sizing, and diversification, can assist in the management of prospective financial losses.

Research and Academic Training:

Keeping up with new information and conducting extensive study are essential for making educated selections when trading. Traders need to keep themselves informed about the latest market movements and economic statistics.

Business Strategy:

Traders can be more successful at sticking to their goals and avoiding impulsive actions if they have a trading plan that is well-defined and includes clear entry and exit methods.

Discipline of the Emotions:

Practices such as meditation, mindfulness, and journaling can help traders cultivate emotional discipline. It is absolutely necessary for long-term success to be able to identify and manage one's emotional reactions.

7.1 Market Volatility and Risk Management

The degree to which the price of a financial instrument fluctuates over the course of time is referred to as market volatility, and it is one of the most important characteristics of financial markets. It is affected by a wide range of elements, including as economic statistics, geopolitical events, the emotion of the market, and the conduct of investors. Volatility, although presenting chances for profit, also poses dangers that traders and investors need to understand and efficiently manage in order to maximize their profits. During this in-depth investigation, we are going to look into the nature of market volatility, its impact on various asset classes, as well as the tactics for effective risk management in markets that are turbulent.

Comprehending the Volatility of the Market

1. **The Characteristics of Volatility in the Market**

   The statistical measure of the dispersion of returns for a particular asset or market index is referred to as market volatility. It is a measure of the degree of risk or uncertainty associated with the price movements of an asset. A higher level of volatility is associated with more significant price swings, whereas a lower level of volatility means that price movements are more steady and may be anticipated.

   The market's reaction to new information is reflected in volatility, as are changes in the supply and demand dynamics, investor attitude, and overall market circumstances. Volatility also reflects changes in overall market conditions.

2. **The Effects That Market Volatility Has**

   The volatility of the market has a significant impact on a variety of asset classes, including currencies, commodities, commodities, and stocks and bonds. High levels of volatility in the equities market can result in significant price changes, prompting investors to reevaluate the investment strategies they have in place. Bond prices and yields can be volatile on the bond market, which can cause interest rate shifts. Volatility also impacts the market overall. The prices of commodities are extremely susceptible to the volatility of the market, which is in turn impacted by the supply-and-demand dynamics, geopolitical events, and macroeconomic factors. The exchange rates that are offered on currency markets are subject to swings, which can have an effect on the flows of international trade and investment.

3. An index of volatility

The Volatility Index, which is more frequently referred to as the VIX, is a well-known measurement of market volatility, particularly for the stock market in the United States. The Chicago Board Options Exchange (CBOE) compiles the VIX, which indicates the expectations of investors regarding the volatility of the market within the following thirty trading days. A greater value for the VIX is indicative of a higher level of predicted volatility, whilst a lower value for the VIX indicates a lower level of expected volatility. The VIX is an important gauge that investors and traders use to evaluate the sentiment of the market as well as the potential threats that the market may face.

Strategies for Risk Management in Markets That Are Volatile

1. **The promotion of diversity**
   The allocation of investments among a variety of asset classes, industries, and geographical areas is what is meant by the term "diversification," which refers to a fundamental risk management technique. Investors can reduce the total risk exposure of their investments and lessen the impact that market volatility has on those holdings by diversifying the holdings in their portfolios. Spreading out one's exposure to risk through diversification can help to improve total risk-adjusted return potential.

2. **Using a hedge**
   The practice of hedging is a method of risk management that entails adopting opposing positions in order to lessen the financial impact of unfavorable market changes. Options, futures contracts, and other derivatives are examples of common hedging tactics.
   These strategies are used to safeguard against potential losses. Through the use of hedging, investors are able to reduce their exposure to potential losses while keeping their exposure to potential gains.

3. **Orders to prevent further loss**
   Stop-loss orders are instructions that investors provide to their brokers to sell a certain security once the price of that security hits a predetermined level. These orders allow for the automated execution of a sell of an asset if the price of that asset swings in a negative direction. This helps to keep potential losses to a minimum. Stop-loss orders are absolutely necessary for safeguarding assets from major risks to the downside, and they are able to be modified according to an investor's comfort level with risk and their investment goals.

4. **Positioning of the Sizes**
   The process of finding the proper amount of capital to allot to a particular transaction or investment is referred to as "position sizing," and it is a part of the discipline of quantitative analysis. Investors can manage their exposure to

market volatility and limit the possible losses they incur by regulating the size of their positions with great care. When dealing with unpredictable markets, it is essential to use conservative position sizing in order to protect capital and avoid experiencing severe drawdowns.

5. **Distribution of Assets**

The process of strategic asset allocation entails putting together a diversified portfolio that is in line with an investor's comfort level with risk and their long-term monetary objectives. Investors can better control their risk exposure and take advantage of a wider range of market possibilities if their assets are spread out across a variety of asset classes. Some of these asset classes include equities, fixed income, and alternative investments. The investor's risk profile and the market conditions should be reassessed on a regular basis, and the asset allocation strategy should be examined and altered accordingly.

6. **Analysis of Both the Fundamentals and the Market**

In order to make educated decisions about investments in turbulent markets, it is necessary to carry out comprehensive fundamental and technical analysis. The process of determining the true worth of an asset by analyzing its past financial results, current market conditions, and historical economic indicators is known as fundamental analysis. The goal of technical analysis is to uncover patterns and trends by doing a study of historical data including price and volume. Combining the two strategies can result in a more comprehensive understanding of the dynamics of the market and can be of assistance in locating prospective investment opportunities.

7. **Conducting a Risk Analysis and Making Contingency Plans**

Evaluating one's own level of comfort with risk and planning for several possible outcomes are two essential aspects of good risk management in unpredictable markets. Investors are able to build contingency plans and set investing goals that are more realistic if they first determine their level of comfort with risk and the potential impact of unfavorable market conditions. Evaluation of a number of possible futures for the market and the formulation of plans to protect against conceivable losses and make the most of attainable gains are both components of scenario planning.

8. **Maintaining a Constant Observation and Course Correction**

It is vital to continuously analyze both the performance of one's portfolio and the conditions of the market in order to successfully adjust to shifting market dynamics. Investors should routinely evaluate their investing plans, determine the effect that market volatility has on their portfolios, and change their risk management tactics as necessary. It is essential, in order to keep a sustainable investment portfolio, to keep up with market trends and incorporate input into the decision-making process.

The financial markets are characterized by an intrinsic quality known as market volatility, which provides investors and traders with both possibilities and risks. Investors are able to handle tumultuous market situations and make informed investment decisions if they have a thorough understanding of the nature of market volatility and put good risk management measures into practice. A comprehensive approach to risk management must include critical components such as diversification, hedging, stop-loss orders, position sizing, asset allocation, fundamental and technical research, risk assessment, and continual monitoring. A disciplined and proactive investing approach that takes into consideration the unpredictability of the market, protects money while simultaneously looking for possible investment opportunities is necessary for effective risk management in markets that are prone to volatility.

7.2 Regulatory Challenges

Regulatory issues are a ubiquitous and essential part of many different industries, including the financial services industry, the healthcare industry, the technology industry, the energy industry, and others. Regulations are put in place to safeguard the general populace, promote honest and open competition, and preserve order in a global environment that is always shifting. This in-depth investigation digs at the regulatory problems that are encountered by individuals, businesses, and governments. We will investigate the difficulty of regulatory frameworks, new developments on a worldwide scale, and the effect that regulatory compliance has on enterprises.

Comprehending the Obstacles Presented by Regulations

1. **The Complicated Nature of the Regulatory Framework**

   The regulatory environment can be broken down into three categories: the local, the national, and the international levels. Each category contains its own unique set of rules, laws, and standards. To comply with severe financial regulations, financial firms confront one set of obstacles; to comply with patient privacy laws, healthcare companies have a different set of challenges. Different sectors and businesses face different regulatory challenges. Compliance may be a challenging endeavor for organizations because of the sheer number and variety of the regulations that must be followed.

2. **The Variability of Regulations**

   In the modern, globalized world, the existence of regulatory differences is a considerable challenge. Countries and regions all have their own regulations and standards, which frequently results in needs that are in direct opposition to one another. The process of harmonizing compliance across many countries is a challenging undertaking for global organizations. Differences in legislation can be a barrier to both international trade and the expansion of the economy.

3. **Swift Progress in the Field of Technology**

As technological advances are made, regulatory frameworks need to be modified to accommodate newly arising problems. The financial technology industry, cryptocurrency, and artificial intelligence are at the forefront of worries over regulatory oversight. The regulatory agencies have to find a middle ground between stifling innovation and overprotecting the public. Rapid technical improvements often occur at a faster rate than the creation of relevant rules, which can result in compliance gaps.

Principal Regulatory Obstacles Faced by All Industries

1. **Services in the Financial Sector**
   The purpose of several financial laws, including Basel III and the Dodd-Frank Act, is to improve the predictability and openness of the financial system. On the other hand, compliance demands significant resources and has the potential to hinder innovation. Financial institutions are tasked with navigating these problems while simultaneously meeting severe standards regarding capital and risk management.

2. **Health care services**
   Regulations governing healthcare, such as the Health Insurance Portability and Accountability Act (HIPAA) in the United States, stipulate stringent requirements for the protection of patient information. Healthcare providers face continual problems, including those related to the management of electronic health records and the maintenance of compliance with privacy rules.

3. **The use of modern technology**
   Concerns such as data privacy, cyber security, and compliance with antitrust legislation are prevalent in the technology industry. In order to prevent antitrust violations, businesses have the challenging task of walking a narrow line between monetizing data and protecting the privacy of their customers.

4. **Environmental Concerns and Energy**
   Companies are required to minimize their carbon emissions in accordance with environmental legislation such as the Paris Agreement, which also encourages the adoption of sustainable business practices. Compliance can require expensive investments in environmentally friendly technologies and activities that offset carbon emissions.

5. **Protection of the Consumers**

Consumer protection rules, such as the General Data Protection Regulation (GDPR) enacted by the European Union, have the objective of empowering individuals by providing them with control over their personal data. Organizations that conduct business on a worldwide scale have a unique set of challenges when attempting to conform to these standards.

Emerging Trends in Regulatory Policy

1. **Regulations Regarding ESG**

   Environmental, Social, and Governance rules (often known as ESG regulations) are gaining more and more importance. Governments and investors are putting pressure on businesses to take greater responsibility in a variety of areas, including ethical governance, social fairness, and climate change. In order for organizations to satisfy these ever-evolving criteria, they are now burdened with the responsibility of monitoring, reporting, and improving their ESG performance.

2. **Regulations Regarding Cryptocurrency and the Blockchain**

   As cryptocurrency and blockchain technologies continue to attract the interest of the general public, regulatory authorities are working to address possible dangers and preserve financial stability. Developing all-encompassing policies that encourage innovation while also reducing instances of fraud and money laundering is a difficult and time-consuming task.

3. **Regulations Concerning the Privacy of Data**

   Data privacy policies are constantly being updated, and stronger rules are being put into place all around the world. In many parts of the world, the protection of one's personal information has been elevated to the status of a fundamental human right. In order to adapt to these ever-evolving requirements, organizations need to ensure the safety of sensitive data and respond appropriately to data breaches.

4. **Regulations Regarding Cybersecurity**

   The rise in the severity of cyberattacks has led to an increase in the number of legislation governing cybersecurity. These safeguards are designed to protect sensitive data, vital infrastructure, and individual privacy. In order for organizations to remain in compliance with these ever-evolving laws, they will need to strengthen their cybersecurity procedures.

5. **Rules Governing Work Done From a Distance**

The COVID-19 pandemic hastened the move toward more jobs that can be done remotely. This transition has given rise to conversations concerning the legislation that govern remote work, including labor laws, the implications of tax law, and data security.

The Effects of Being in Compliance with Regulations

1. **The Costs of Compliance**

   Regulatory compliance frequently necessitates the expenditure of considerable amounts of money. Businesses are required to set aside funds for the hiring of legal counsel, the implementation of regulatory technology (RegTech), and employee training. These charges can put a strain on a company's budget, especially for those businesses classified as small and medium-sized (SMEs).

2. **An Advantage Over the Competition**
   The ability to comply with regulations can provide a source of competitive advantage. Consumers and investors who are socially conscious may be attracted to businesses that embrace ethical business methods, sustainable business practices, and data protection. It is possible to improve an organization's reputation by showing that it is committed to compliance.

3. **Dangers to One's Reputation and Legal Standing**
   Failure to comply carries risks, both legally and in terms of one's reputation. Infractions of
   regulations can lead to financial penalties, criminal prosecution, and a tarnished reputation for an institution. It is really necessary for companies to comprehend these dangers and implement efficient compliance systems in order to lessen their impact.

4. **Creativity and Flexible Adaptation**

Innovation can be sparked by difficult regulatory requirements. Businesses frequently come up with inventive ways to satisfy the standards of compliance while simultaneously boosting efficiency and enhancing operations. It is possible for an organization to become more resilient and competitive if it adapts to newly enacted legislation.

Methods for Conquering the Obstacles Presented by Regulations

1. **Regulatory Technology, Abbreviated as "RegTech"**
   The application of technology within RegTech solutions assists businesses in more effectively complying with regulations. Using these tools, compliance activities may be automated, changes in rules can be monitored, and compliance-related data can be managed. Keeping one step ahead of ever-evolving regulatory requirements is impossible without the assistance of RegTech.

2. **Teams in Charge of Legal and Compliance Matters**
   When it comes to interpreting and carrying out the requirements of regulations, having a legal and compliance staff on hand is absolutely necessary. These specialists make certain that the organization is aware of its responsibilities and continues to comply with regulations. Working together with regulatory challenge managers who are knowledgeable in legal matters is a good strategy.

3. **Ongoing Instruction and Instructional Programs**
   It is absolutely necessary to keep up to date on any regulatory changes. Employees benefit from ongoing education and training, which helps develop their awareness of compliance issues and their level of competency in dealing with them. Keeping up to date with the latest advancements in regulatory requirements can help firms adjust more swiftly.

4. **Cooperation Between Businesses**

   Working together with others in the same industry, as well as industry groups and regulators, can yield useful insights and recommendations for best practices in the management of regulatory difficulties. Industry networks can assist firms in collaboratively navigating the ever-changing regulatory landscape.

5. **Structures for the Management of Risk**

It is absolutely necessary to construct solid frameworks for risk management. Identifying, evaluating, and taking measures to mitigate compliance risks should be an inherent component of the strategy planning process for every firm.

The present landscape of business is inherently fraught with difficulties caused by regulations. The complexity of regulatory frameworks, the emergence of new trends, and the management of the impact of regulatory compliance are all challenges that organizations need to overcome. Businesses are able to traverse regulatory difficulties more effectively if they use RegTech solutions, establish educated legal and compliance teams, provide continuous education and training, foster industry collaboration, and put strong risk management frameworks into place. Organizations that make compliance their first priority in a regulatory environment that is constantly evolving are in a stronger position to succeed while still living up to their commitments to society, consumers, and investors.

7.3 Ethical Concerns and Insider Trading

The practice of engaging in insider trading has, for an extended period of time, been the source of substantial ethical concerns in the world of finance and investment. People who have access to confidential, non-public information about a company may engage in insider trading when they use that information to make financial gains for themselves by purchasing or selling the firm's stocks. This practice is commonly seen as unethical, as well as illegal, and as being detrimental to the integrity of the financial markets. During this in-depth investigation, we will look into the ethical considerations that surround insider trading, as well as its ramifications for financial markets, the legal system that is supposed to prevent it, and the current disputes over its enforcement and the repercussions of engaging in it.

Comprehending the Practice of Insider Trading

1. **The Meaning of the Term "Insider Trading"**

   Insider trading is when a person buys or sells a security while in possession of material, non-public knowledge about the security, in violation of a fiduciary responsibility or other relationship of trust and confidence. This occurs while the person is in possession of confidential information.

   Because insiders use their position of informational advantage to further their own financial interests, this conduct violates the concept that all participants in the financial markets should have fair and equal access to information.

2. **Different Categories of Insider Trading**

There are two primary types of insider trading, and they are as follows:
Insider Trading That Is Allowed by the Law Trading on the Inside of a Company That Is Allowed by the Law entails transactions carried out by company insiders, such as executives and employees, that are fully declared and adhere to regulatory rules. These people have a legal obligation to disclose their dealings to both the relevant authorities and the general public. Buying and selling shares can be considered forms of legal insider trading so long as the transactions are carried out in accordance with all applicable laws and regulations.

Illegal Insider Trading Unauthorized trading of a security on the basis of significant information that is not readily available to the public is an example of illegal insider trading. This specific form of trading on inside information is the principal focus of ethical issues and is subject to legal consequences.

Concerns Regarding Ethical Implications of Insider Trading

1. **Advantage Gained Unfairly**
   The unfair advantage that insider trading provides to individuals who are in possession of non-public information is one of the most significant ethical concerns raised by the practice. Common investors do not have access to this information and hence are unable to make decisions about their investments that are informed. As a consequence of this, insider trading undermines the fundamental principle of market fairness, which states that all market participants ought to have the same level of access to relevant information.

2. **Breach of the Trust and Confidence Obligation**
   Executives and other workers of a company have a responsibility to act in the best interests of the company's shareholders. They are obligated to make decisions that are in the best interests of the firm as well as the shareholders who own it. Trading on inside information constitutes a breach of this fiduciary duty since those involved put their own financial benefit ahead of their responsibility to the company's shareholders and other stakeholders.

3. **The deterioration of faith**
   The financial markets are built on a foundation of trust. When insider trading takes place, it erodes trust in the integrity of the markets, as investors may become doubtful of the fairness and transparency of the trading system. This can have a negative impact on the economy as a whole. This mistrust can lead to inefficiencies in the market and a reduction in the participation of investors.

4. **Manipulation of the Market**

Insider trading can lead to market manipulation since the unlawful publication of non-public information can artificially inflate or deflate the price of a security.

This can be done by either driving up or driving down demand for the asset. This manipulation has the potential to cause harm to other investors and skew the market's accurate valuation of assets.

The Existing Legal Structure and Its Enforcement

1. **The Securities and Exchange Commission, most often known as the SEC**
   The Securities and Exchange Commission, sometimes known as the SEC, is the major regulatory organization in the United States that is responsible for implementing the regulations against insider trading. The Securities and Exchange Commission (SEC) mandates that corporate insiders declare their transactions and then makes this information available to the general public through various forms, such as Form 4. In addition to this, the agency investigates and prosecutes unlawful conduct involving insider trading.

2. **Legislation that forbids engaging in "insider trading"**
   There are a number of laws in the United States that make it specifically illegal to engage in insider trading. The Securities Exchange Act of 1934 and Rule 10b-5 are the most prominent of these laws because they make it illegal to engage in fraudulent or misleading conduct in connection with securities trading. These laws are among the most important of these laws. In addition, the Insider Trading and Securities Fraud Enforcement Act of 1988 raised the penalty for violators of the rules governing insider trading.

3. **Regulation on a Global Scale**

Regulations on insider trading can vary greatly from one nation to the next, each with its own unique legal structure and set of enforcement methods. While there is a constant adherence to the fundamental principle of barring trading based on material non-public information, the exact laws and penalties for breaking this rule vary. When addressing instances of insider trading that occur across international borders, international collaboration and the sharing of information have become increasingly vital.

Obstacles to Compliance and Enforcement

1. **Convincing Evidence of Insider Trading**
   It can be difficult to prove that an individual engaged in illegal insider trading. It is necessary for the prosecution to present evidence that the accused have access to material non-public information, that they traded on this knowledge, and that they did so intentionally and with the purpose to deceive in order to secure convictions. It may be challenging to collect adequate evidence in order to fulfill these requirements.

2. **Reconnaissance**
   Another difficult task is identifying instances of insider trading in real time. The identification of potential infractions is the responsibility of regulatory agencies,

and these organizations rely on tips, whistleblowers, and market surveillance systems. However, not every incidence is discovered, and some persons may go undiscovered for years at a time.

3. **The International Character of the Financial Markets**

The fact that financial markets are conducted on a worldwide scale makes enforcement measures more difficult. Because insider trading might involve participants from a variety of nations, it can be difficult to coordinate investigations and transfer information amongst parties. Consistency in legislation and punishments must be maintained across international borders, which is a continuous difficulty.

Ongoing Discussions

1. **An Explanation of What Is Considered Important Information**
   The question of what constitutes "material information" is one that is still being discussed. It is not always easy to determine what constitutes material information, and the answer can change based on the circumstances. Because of this uncertainty, it can be difficult to prosecute cases, and it may also lead to varying views of what constitutes unlawful insider trading and what does not.

2. **Preventive Measures and Punitive Consequences**
   Some people believe that the consequences for engaging in insider trading are not severe enough to prevent people from engaging in illegal behavior. Some people believe that more severe punishments might be more successful in preventing illicit insider trading. The question of how to find a middle ground between punitive measures and preventative measures is still being discussed.

3. **Protection for People Who Whistleblower**

In the process of bringing insider trading to light, whistleblowers are an extremely valuable resource. The subject of the argument is how to best shield and reward people who blow the whistle on wrongdoing. It is very necessary, in order to preserve the integrity of the market, to provide sufficient protections and rewards for those persons who report illicit actions.

Fairness, trustworthiness, and maintaining the integrity of the market are the cornerstones of the ethical considerations that accompany insider trading. Unauthorized trading on the basis of important non-public information violates the fiduciary obligation of the company and undermines the fundamental principles of transparency and fairness in the financial markets. Legal frameworks, such as the Securities Exchange Act of 1934 in the United States, try to prevent unlawful insider trading and penalize those who engage in it. In spite of this, enforcement continues to be difficult, particularly in the current globalized and technologically complex financial sector.

The definition of "material information," the efficacy of fines as a deterrent, and the protection and incentivizing of whistleblowers are at the center of the ongoing arguments around insider trading. The complexity of addressing the ethical considerations associated to insider trading and the ongoing attempts to safeguard the integrity of financial markets has been brought into sharp relief by these disputes. In the end, addressing these problems and maintaining the credibility and integrity of financial systems around the world requires a strong emphasis on openness, enforcement, and ethical awareness.

7.4 The Impact of Global Economic Events

The economies, financial markets, enterprises, and individuals all around the world are profoundly and significantly impacted by the events that occur on the global economic stage. These occurrences, which can take the form of anything from a geopolitical battle to a financial crisis, frequently set off dramatic shifts in economic indicators, the behavior of markets, and policy decisions. In the course of this investigation, we will investigate the myriad of ways in which current events affecting the global economy have an effect on the current economic landscape.

Important Economic Events from a Global Perspective

1. **Problems with the economy**

   Significant occurrences in the world economy include calamities on the financial markets, such as the global financial crisis of 2008 and the Asian financial crisis of 1997. In the majority of cases, these crises are characterized by the failure of financial institutions, the crash of stock markets, and substantial disruptions in credit markets.

   They influence economies all around the world, causing a domino effect in the process. In response to financial instability, governments and central banks frequently implement measures to stabilize financial systems. These actions might take the shape of stimulus packages, changes in interest rates, or regulatory reforms.

2. **Conflicts Regarding Trade**

   Global supply chains can be negatively impacted by trade disputes and tariff wars, which can also impair international trade. The ongoing trade disputes between the United States and China, for example, have had an influence worldwide, leading to alterations in global trade patterns and affecting industries ranging from manufacturing to agriculture. This is just one example of the global repercussions of these tensions.

3. **Political Conflicts and Internationally Significant Occurrences**

   Uncertainty can be exacerbated in global markets as a result of geopolitical events such as crises in the Middle East or tensions between major countries. These occurrences may have an effect on the price of oil, cause a disruption in international relations, and cause people to flee with their money. Sanctions and trade embargoes can be the direct result of geopolitical crises, which can then have a domino effect on other economies.

4. **Catastrophic Natural Events**

   Natural disasters, such as earthquakes, hurricanes, and pandemics, have economic repercussions not only in the immediate area, but also on a global scale. These occurrences have the potential to cause immediate damage to infrastructure, wreak havoc on supply networks, and have an effect on the insurance and reinsurance industries. For example, the COVID-19 pandemic was responsible for economic shocks around the world as a result of its extensive repercussions on both health and the economy.

5. **Significant Shifts in Policy**

Changes in monetary policy, changes in fiscal policy, or changes in regulatory policies can all have repercussions on the international stage. For instance, the decision made by central banks to change interest rates or to carry out quantitative easing can have an effect on currency exchange rates, investment flows, and the sentiment of global financial markets.

Influence on Different Economic Indicators

1. **The Rates of Exchange**

   Currency exchange rates are susceptible to major movement as a result of economic events on a global scale.

   Changes in economic conditions, interest rates, and political stability can frequently be shown to have an effect on currency values. For example, when there is a great deal of economic unpredictability, investors may want to find safety in safe-haven currencies such as the United States dollar. This can have an effect on the exchange values of other currencies.

2. **The Stock Exchanges**

   The stock market is frequently volatile as a result of significant economic events that occur around the world. Changes in economic statistics, such as gross domestic product growth, unemployment rates, and corporate earnings, elicit responses from investors. Uncertainty brought on by events such as financial crises can lead to panic selling, which in turn can cause sharp losses in market value.

3. **The Cost of Basic Materials**

   The prices of commodities, such as oil, gold, and agricultural items, are highly reactive to changes in economic conditions around the world. For example, a sudden reduction in oil supply as a result of geopolitical conflicts can lead to increasing oil prices, which in turn affects the cost of energy for industries and consumers all over the world.

4. **The Current Interest Rates**

   Interest rates are also affected by the state of the global economy. Adjustments to interest rates made by central banks in response to changes in economic conditions have the effect of having a knock-on effect on the prices that firms and consumers pay for borrowing money. When it comes to economic growth, having lower interest rates can be beneficial, while having higher rates can help bring inflation under control.

5. **The Flow of Trade**

Trade disputes and geopolitical tensions are examples of global economic events that can have an impact on the volumes and patterns of international trade. These events have the potential to disrupt established trade connections and lead to changes in imports and exports, which will have an effect on the economies of the nations concerned as well as the economies of their trading partners.

Influence felt by local companies

1. **Disruptions in the Supply Chain**
   Events that occur on a global economic scale can wreak havoc on supply systems. Interruption in production and distribution of products and services has been brought on by a variety of factors, including natural catastrophes, trade tensions, and pandemics.
   Businesses are required to adjust to these shifts and look for new ways to source their supplies and organize their logistics.
2. **The Management of Risk**
   The risk faced by businesses can be dramatically impacted by economic events. For example, organizations that engage in international trade are exposed to risks associated with fluctuating currency exchange rates. Hedging and diversification are two examples of risk management strategies that are frequently utilized by businesses in order to lessen the negative effects of various hazards.
3. **Adjustments to the Regulations**

Events that occur on a global economic scale might result in regulatory changes, which can have an effect on the operations of firms and the needs for compliance. For instance, regulatory improvements in the banking and financial sectors frequently follow in the wake of financial crises. These reforms result in heightened scrutiny and compliance duties.

Influence on the Lives of Individuals

1. **Obtaining a Job**
   Events that occur on a global economic scale can have an effect on employment chances. Downturns in the economy can lead to job losses, while economic booms can lead to an increase in the number of jobs being created. It may be necessary for individuals to adjust to the shifting conditions of the labor market and look for possibilities in a variety of industries.

2. **Sources of Revenue and Wealth**

   The income and wealth of individuals can be influenced by economic events. Changes in interest rates can have an impact on savings accounts and retirement funds, while falls in the value of the stock market can eat away at the value of investment portfolios. A worsening of economic disparity is another possibility during times of economic crisis.

3. **Average Monthly Expenditure**

Changes in the cost of living may be brought about by occurrences in the global economy. For instance, an increase in the price of oil can lead to an increase in the price of gasoline and in monthly energy bills, which can have an influence on household finances. As a result of these developments, individuals might need to make adjustments to the ways in which they spend money and organize their finances.

The Reaction of the Government

1. **The Role of Monetary Policy**

   To exert influence over the current state of the economy and the financial markets, central banks may make changes to the interest rate structure, engage in quantitative easing, or participate in currency exchange markets.

2. **The Budget and Finances**

   Stimulating economic growth and providing assistance to individuals and businesses during times of economic depression can be accomplished by governments through the employment of fiscal policy measures such as tax cuts, increased government expenditure, and stimulus packages.

3. **The Commercial Policy**

   Protecting domestic industries or addressing trade imbalances created by global economic events may require governments to negotiate trade agreements, apply tariffs, or give subsidies. These options are all available to governments.

4. **Changes to Existing Regulations**

Economic developments on a global scale can serve as a catalyst for regulatory changes that solve weaknesses in financial markets, provide protections for consumers, and strengthen the economy as a whole.

The current state of the world's economy is a facet of the modern world that is both pervasive and influential. In a myriad of different ways, they have an effect on economies, financial markets, businesses, and individuals. These events have the potential to cause disruptions to supply chains, variations in exchange values, and volatility in stock markets, as well as changes in interest rates. Businesses and individuals alike will need to adjust to these shifts, while governments will need to take action in the areas of monetary, fiscal, and trade policy to reduce the negative effects.

If you want to make educated choices as an investor, a business owner, or a policy-maker, it is essential to have a solid understanding of the interrelated nature of the global economy as well as the potential repercussions that could result from economic events. Individuals and organizations are able to negotiate the obstacles that are provided by the events that occur on a global scale and seize chances for growth and prosperity if they remain informed, engage in risk management practices that are wise, and remain adaptable in the face of uncertainty.

Chapter 8

Trading and Social Development

Trading, a fundamental economic activity that stretches back millennia, has played a crucial role in the route that human history has taken, as well as the progression of society. Trading has not only made the interchange of commodities and services easier over the course of human history, but it has also made significant contributions to the growth of society in a variety of different ways. This in-depth investigation digs into the dynamic relationship between trading and social evolution. It investigates the ways in which trading practices, procedures, and inventions have influenced social structures, cultural exchange, economic empowerment, and global interconnectedness. In addition, we will study the impact that social growth has had on business, focusing on the ways in which inclusion, sustainability, and ethical considerations have played a part in the formation of contemporary business practices.

Perspectives on the Role of Commerce in the Evolution of Society Throughout History

1. **Commercial Networks and the Spread of Culture**
   In the course of human history, trade routes such as the Silk Road, the Trans-Saharan trade routes, and the Maritime Silk Road made it easier for people from different civilizations to interact culturally and to share ideas, faiths, and technology with one another. These encounters encouraged the sharing of knowledge, languages, and cultural practices, which contributed to the creation of a wide variety of communities that are today interrelated.

2. **Empowerment of the Economic Underclass and Urbanization**
   The expansion of economic activity and the emergence of urban areas have both been significantly aided by commercial trading. The development of market-places, trading hubs, and commercial centers has facilitated economic empowerment and social mobility by encouraging the concentration of populations, the rise of cities, and the emergence of specialized professions and trades. This has led to the growth of cities worldwide.

3. **The Development of Various Institutions and Trading Networks**

In order to facilitate organized trading activities, ensure the enforcement of trade agreements, and promote standardization in commercial procedures, the establishment of trading networks and organizations, such as guilds, trading firms, and stock exchanges, has been essential. These institutions have been extremely important in the process of forming the framework of economies as well as societies.

During the Modern Era, Commercial Activity Contributed to the Growth of Society

1. **The growth of globalization and interdependence**
   The expansion of global trade and the number of interconnected societies has been hastened in the modern period by developments in transportation, communications, and digital technology. The expansion of market access, the facilitation of the exchange of ideas and cultures, and the promotion of international collaboration have all contributed to the growth of a global community as a result of globalization.
2. **The Elimination of Poverty and the Promotion of Economic Empowerment**
   Trading has the potential to drive economic empowerment and to reduce poverty to some degree. Trading activities have the potential to create employment opportunities, produce revenue, and enhance living standards, particularly in economies that are still in the process of growing; they do this by facilitating access to foreign markets; permitting the export of goods and services; and encouraging entrepreneurial activity.
3. **Ethical Business Practices and Long-Term Sustainability**

In recent years, there has been a growing emphasis placed on the incorporation of ethical and environmentally responsible business practices into commercial transactions. Trading practices are increasingly aligning with the principles of sustainability, social responsibility, and ethical supply chain management, contributing to the well-being of communities and the preservation of natural resources. This emphasis on the environment, fair trade, and responsible sourcing is driving this alignment.

The Influence That Changing Social Conditions Have On Business Practices

1. **Commercial Practices That Are Open To All Parties**
   The advancement of inclusive trading policies, such as preferential trade agreements, tariff reductions for developing countries, and support for small and medium-sized enterprises (SMEs), has contributed to the diversification of trading partnerships, the empowerment of marginalized communities, and the promotion of equitable economic growth. These goals have been accomplished through the promotion of inclusive trading policies.

2. **The rise of digitalization and online business**
   Trading methods have been changed as a result of advancements in digitalization and the widespread adoption of e-commerce platforms. These developments have made it possible for firms to reach a global client base, streamline operations along the supply chain, and promote financial inclusion. The implementation of digital technology has increased market accessibility and stoked the fires of economic growth in both urban and suburban locations.

3. **Initiatives Regarding Corporate Social Responsibility (also Called CSR)**

CSR (Corporate Social Responsibility) projects that stress social welfare, community development, and environmental sustainability are gaining increased support from corporate entities. Companies are developing a culture of ethical commerce and contributing to the well-being of societies by incorporating responsible business practices, promoting transparency, and providing financial support for social development programs.

The Obstacles and Opportunities Faced in Commercial Trade Regarding Social Development

1. **Unequal distribution of income and unequal access to trade**
   The ongoing existence of wealth inequality and unequal access to possibilities in commerce both present obstacles to the progression of social life. The economic advancement of excluded populations can be hampered, in addition to attempts to promote inclusive and sustainable development, by restrictions on trade, market barriers, and trade, as well as limited access to resources.

2. **Environmental deterioration and environmentally responsible business practices**
   Significant obstacles to social progress are presented by the expansion of practices in trade that are not sustainable, the depletion of resources, and the pollution of the environment. It is vital to incorporate models of circular economies, promote environmentally friendly projects, and adopt sustainable trade practices in order to reduce the negative effects that commercial transactions have on the surrounding environment.

3. **Concerns With Regard To Ethical Practices And Fair Trade Standards**
   Concerns pertaining to ethics, such as the exploitation of labor, breaches of human rights, and unethical business practices in supply chains, continue to pose a threat to the integrity of trading systems. The promotion of social justice, the protection of worker rights, and the assurance of the ethical sourcing of goods and services are all dependent on the establishment of fair trade standards, the promotion of transparency, and the enforcement of ethical rules.

4. **Technological Inequalities and the Gap between the Digital and Analog Worlds**

Disparities in technology and the digital divide are two factors that can make it difficult for underserved populations to participate in global commerce networks. For the purpose of providing fair access to trading opportunities and increasing social development, closing the digital divide, encouraging the spread of digital literacy, and making investments in technology infrastructure are crucial.

The Way Forward: Creating a Trading Landscape That Is Both Sustainable and Inclusive

1. **Economic Strategies That Include All Parties**
   Trade policies that are inclusive should be prioritized by governments, international organizations, and trade groups. These policies should eliminate trade barriers, assist small and medium-sized enterprises (SMEs), and provide particular considerations for communities that are marginalized. Trade agreements ought to be fashioned in such a way as to guarantee fair participation in the international trading system.

2. **Methods of Conducting Ethical Business**
   Encouragement of sustainable business practices should come in the form of financial incentives, government legislation, and voluntary industry standards. While governments and international organizations should encourage environmentally responsible trade policies, businesses should embrace ecologically responsible practices for sourcing, production, and distribution of their products.

3. **Initiatives Regarding Ethical Trading**
   It is imperative that businesses and governments take decisive action to eradicate unethical business practices and ensure that fair trade principles are adhered to. This involves conducting ethical labor practices, conducting transparent reporting on social and environmental implications, and maintaining stringent monitoring of supplier chains.

4. **Participation in the Digital Age**
   It is necessary to make efforts to bridge the digital divide and promote digital inclusion if we want to guarantee that underserved communities will be able to engage in e-commerce and other types of digital trade platforms. Among the most important aspects of this initiative are financial commitments to the development of digital infrastructure, educational activities in the area of digital literacy, and expanded access to affordable technology.

5. **Investing in Educational Opportunities and Professional Growth**

It is essential to make investments in education and the development of skills in order to give individuals and communities the ability to actively participate in commercial activity. Programs that teach relevant skills, provide vocational education, and encourage entrepreneurialism can boost economic prospects and contribute to the growth of society.

The connection between economic exchange and the progress of societies is complex and takes on many different forms. Throughout the course of history, the act of trading goods and services has served as a primary catalyst for the spread of new cultures, the development of cities, and the acceleration of economic growth. It is currently playing a crucial part in the modern era in the promotion of globalization, economic empowerment, and long-term sustainability. On the other hand, the evolution of society has had an impact on business practices by way of defining legislation, supporting digitalization, and fostering ethical issues.

It is essential to address difficulties such as income inequality, environmental degradation, ethical concerns, and technological gaps in order to take use of the potential that trading has for contributing to social progress. Trading practices that are both sustainable and inclusive, in conjunction with trade policies that are inclusive, have the potential to contribute to a more equitable and prosperous world. Trading and social growth are ultimately inextricably linked, and the nature of the interaction between the two is constantly shifting in response to shifts in economic paradigms, technical paradigms, and ethical paradigms.

8.1 Trading's Role in Infrastructure Projects

Trading plays an essential part in the planning and implementation of infrastructure projects, which in turn acts as a driver of economic expansion, the production of new jobs, and the furtherance of societal progress. Construction of transportation networks, energy facilities, telecommunications systems, and public utility systems are all examples of the diverse types of projects that fall under the umbrella term "infrastructure projects." These projects call for significant investments, as well as resources and skills, all of which can be facilitated through effective trading networks and systems. During this extensive investigation, we will look into the multidimensional function that trading plays in infrastructure projects. Specifically, we will investigate the impact that trading has on project financing, the acquisition of resources, and worldwide collaboration. In addition, we will conduct an analysis of the potential and difficulties connected with trade in the development of infrastructure, with a particular focus on the significance of environmentally responsible business practices, advances in technology, and efficient risk management measures.

The Importance of Commercial Activity in the Construction of Infrastructure

1. **Investment and Financing Options for Projects**

   Trading is an extremely important part of the process of developing infrastructure since it helps to facilitate project finance and investment. Trading mechanisms are relied on by financial institutions, investors, and government bodies to manage the financial risks involved with large-scale infrastructure projects, as well as to raise cash, get loans, and arrange financing. Trading permits the mobilization of resources that are necessary for the successful implementation of infrastructure initiatives. These resources can be gathered through the sale of bonds, the signing of project finance agreements, and the formation of public-private partnerships.

2. **Management of the Supply Chain and the Acquisition of Resources**
Building new infrastructure necessitates the utilization of a wide variety of resources, such as laborers with specialized skills, construction materials, and various pieces of machinery. Trading networks make it easier to acquire these resources through global supply chains, which in turn makes it possible for supplies to be delivered to construction sites in an effective and on-time manner. It is necessary to have efficient supply chain management that is backed by trading practices in order to guarantee the continual flow of resources, minimize project delays, and keep costs from spiraling out of control.

3. **International Cooperation and the Spreading of Knowledge**

The promotion of global collaboration and the exchange of information through trading is beneficial to the development of infrastructure. Sharing of best practices, technical advances, and engineering skills across national boundaries is made possible through the formation of international partnerships and collaborations. These coordinated efforts contribute to the application of innovative building practices, the development of environmentally responsible infrastructure solutions, and the improvement of the overall productivity and quality of the project.

The Function of Trading in the Various Infrastructure Sectors

1. **Facilities for Travel and Transportation**
Transportation infrastructure, such as roads, bridges, airports, and trains, was largely developed thanks in large part to the contributions made by the trading industry. Trading networks make it easier to acquire construction materials, machinery, and specialized equipment, which helps to ensure that transportation projects are finished on schedule and to a high standard. In addition, commerce contributes to the development of international trade routes and logistical networks, which in turn promotes economic integration and connectedness on a worldwide scale.

2. **Infrastructure for the Energy Sector**
Trading is an essential component of the growth of power plants, renewable energy facilities, and transmission networks in the energy sector. Trading activities make it possible to acquire the raw materials, components, and technology needed for energy infrastructure projects. This helps contribute to the diversity of energy sources, the expansion of access to energy, and the development of sustainable energy solutions.

3. **The Infrastructure of the Telecommunications Industry**
Trading is a crucial component in the growth of telecommunications infrastructure, which includes the building of fiber-optic networks, satellite

communication systems, and digital connectivity solutions. Specifically, these developments cannot occur without trading. Trading mechanisms make it easier to acquire telecommunications equipment, technology components, and software, which in turn helps to support the growth of digital connectivity, the improvement of communication networks, and the promotion of technical innovation.

4. The Infrastructure of the Public Utilities

Trading makes it easier to create infrastructure for public utilities such as water supply systems, sewage treatment facilities, and waste management. This is true in the field of public utilities. To ensure the delivery of clean water, the administration of sanitation services, and the promotion of environmental sustainability, it is needed to make purchases of water treatment technologies, materials for pipelines, and waste disposal equipment.

Trading for infrastructure projects presents both a number of challenges and opportunities

1. **The Management of Risk and Delays in Projects**
   Regulatory shifts, geopolitical unpredictability, and environmental obstacles are just some of the potential dangers that might befall infrastructure construction projects. It is absolutely necessary to have efficient risk management techniques in place in order to mitigate potential trading-related risks and reduce the likelihood of project delays. Some examples of such tactics are the diversification of suppliers, the execution of contingency plans, and the adoption of risk-sharing systems.

2. **Sustainable and Ethical Sourcing of Goods and Services**
   For the sake of fostering environmental preservation and social responsibility in infrastructure development, environmentally responsible and ethical purchasing methods are absolutely necessary. Trading entities have a responsibility to comply to sustainability standards, ethical supply chain procedures, and responsible sourcing criteria in order to reduce the environmental impact of infrastructure projects, protect the rights of local communities and workers involved in the supply chain, and minimize the amount of waste generated by the projects.

3. **the incorporation of new technologies and digitalization**
   The panorama of infrastructure development is undergoing a transformation as a result of the integration of cutting-edge technology and digitization. To improve transparency, streamline procurement procedures, and maximize project management in the infrastructure sector, trading organizations need to adopt technology innovations such as digital procurement platforms, blockchain-based supply chain solutions, and predictive analytics.

4. **Compliance with Regulatory Requirements and Alignment of Policies**

It is essential for the successful execution of infrastructure projects to adhere to regulatory compliance and match trading practices with national and international policies. Trading companies have a responsibility to keep ahead of new regulatory frameworks, maintain quality and safety standards, and ensure compliance with procurement requirements in order to avoid the legal ramifications and reputational hazards that are associated with these risks.

The Way Forward: Trading Practices That Are Both Sustainable and Inclusive in the Infrastructure Sector

1. **Methods of Sustainable Purchasing**

   The use of environmentally friendly materials, technologies that are efficient in their use of energy, and supply chain partners that are ethical should be given priority in sustainable procurement procedures. Trading entities involved in infrastructure should conform to sustainability norms, promote models of circular economies, and engage in responsible sourcing in order to reduce their negative effects on the environment.

2. **The Evolution of Digital Technology**

   It is vital to use digital technologies such as e-procurement platforms, real-time tracking systems, and data analytics in order to optimize procurement procedures and enhance transparency in the trading of infrastructure. The use of digital technology increases productivity, lowers operating expenses, and paves the way for the seamless administration of intricate supply chains.

3. **Measures to Reduce the Danger**

   In order to reduce the likelihood of potential trading-related risks in infrastructure projects, efficient risk management measures should be put into action. The timely and cost-effective completion of infrastructure projects can be helped along by utilizing risk-sharing arrangements, a diversified supply chain, and various planning and contingency strategies.

4. **Cooperation on a Global Scale**

Within the infrastructure trade community, there should be a greater emphasis placed on global collaboration and the exchange of expertise. Sharing of best practices, innovative technologies, and engineering experience can be facilitated through international partnerships and cooperation, which contributes to the effective execution of infrastructure projects and the promotion of global connectivity.

Trading is an essential part of the process of developing infrastructure since it acts as a driver for the financing of projects, the acquisition of resources, and the coordination of efforts on a worldwide scale. Trading practices are essential to the effective completion of infrastructure projects in a variety of industries, including transportation, energy, telecommunications, and public utilities. These projects require access to the materials, equipment, and knowledge necessary for their completion.

Trading gives a great number of opportunities for the development of infrastructure; nevertheless, it also presents a number of obstacles in the areas of risk management, sustainability, technological integration, and regulatory compliance. In order to cultivate a resilient and equitable ecosystem for trading in the context of infrastructure development, it is essential to embrace trading methods that are both inclusive and sustainable, to adhere to procurement criteria based on ethical principles, and to embrace digitization.

When it comes to the development of infrastructure, commercial companies, national governments, and international organizations all need to collaborate in order to guarantee the smooth execution of essential infrastructure projects that are necessary for fostering economic expansion, societal progress, and environmental sustainability. The infrastructure industry has the potential to contribute to the development of resilient, egalitarian, and successful societies by placing a higher priority on trading practices that are sustainable and inclusive.

8.2 Education and Skill Development

Education and the cultivation of skills are key drivers of individual and societal progress; they promote economic expansion, social mobility, and international competitiveness. Individuals are provided with the resources essential to succeed in a world that is always changing when they acquire the information, abilities, and skills necessary. During this in-depth investigation, we will delve into the complex relationship that exists between education, skill development, and the progression of society. Specifically, we will investigate the influence that education has on both individual and societal well-being, the importance of skill development in terms of employability, as well as the inherent difficulties and opportunities that are associated with these spheres.

The Influence of a Good Education

1. **Acquiring Information and Developing Your Mind**
   The acquisition of new knowledge and the growth of one's cognitive abilities can be greatly facilitated by education. It enables individuals to develop their critical thinking, problem-solving, and intellectual capacities by providing them with a comprehensive understanding of a variety of topics. Individuals' mental capacities can be improved by the pursuit of education since it exposes them to a wider variety of viewpoints, cultures, and fields of study.

2. **Intelligence in social and emotional situations**
   Education goes beyond the academic realm and helps students develop their social and emotional intelligence. People gain the ability to communicate with their peers, develop empathy for those around them, and form interpersonal relationships through their educational experiences. These competencies are necessary for one's own well-being as well as for success in both professional and social settings.

3. **A Healthy and Thriving Economy**

   On a personal and a societal level, having a good education is one of the most important factors that contributes to economic success. It improves employability as well as work options and the possibility for revenue. Having a workforce that is well educated can lead to increased productivity and creativity, which in turn fuels economic growth and contributes to global competitiveness.

4. **Mobility within Society**

Education is one of the most important factors in determining an individual's social mobility since it provides people with the potential to overcome socio-economic barriers. It offers people a way to enhance their socioeconomic standing, gain access to better work prospects, and make a positive contribution to the development of the communities in which they live.

The Development of Skills as a Stepping Stone Towards Employability

1. **Competencies Required for Today's Workforce**

   Developing one's skills is critical in order to adequately prepare persons for the requirements of today's labor force. Employers value academic knowledge, but they also place a high premium on practical abilities in potential employees. Digital literacy, the capacity to solve problems, communicate effectively, and adaptability are just few of the abilities that are essential in this day and age of rapid technological change.

2. **Capacity for Gainful Employment and Progress in One's Career**

   The development of skills increases employability as well as the potential for career advancement. People who have a varied range of abilities are more marketable in the job market because they are able to switch between different kinds of work and different kinds of industries. They are also in a better position to take advantage of new work chances and advance their careers.

3. **Innovation and entrepreneurial endeavors**

Developing one's skills is essential to both entrepreneurial endeavors and innovative endeavors. Entrepreneurs need a diverse set of talents, ranging from an understanding of business and marketing to the ability to manage projects and understand finances. Individuals who have developed skills to their full potential are able to take chances, generate innovative solutions, and propel economic expansion.

The Obstacles to Overcome and the Potential Benefits

1. **Availability of Good Educational Opportunities**

   One of the difficulties faced in the field of education is ensuring that all students have access to educational opportunities of sufficient quality. Inequalities can be perpetuated and social mobility can be hampered when there are disparities in access to education, particularly in groups that are economically disadvantaged and socially stigmatized. Targeted actions and policies that include everyone need to be implemented by governments and other organizations in order to close this gap.

2. **A Mismatch in Capabilities**

   The term "skills mismatch" refers to a situation in which the abilities possessed by the workforce are not in alignment with the demands of the job market. This situation can lead to both unemployment and underemployment. To effectively address this problem, educational institutions, businesses, and politicians will need to work together to guarantee that education and training programs are tailored to meet the requirements of the job market.

3. **Education that lasts a lifetime**

   The rapid rate of technology advancement necessitates a shift toward learning that continues throughout one's life. To maintain their value in the labor market, individuals are required to continually expand their skill sets. It is essential for both individual and social growth to foster a culture of learning that lasts a lifetime, one that is supported by educational opportunities that are both accessible and adaptable.

4. **Differences Between the Sexes**

There are still significant gender gaps in terms of education and the development of skills in many parts of the world. Women frequently confront obstacles that prevent them from gaining access to school and improving their skills, hence reducing the options available to them for economic empowerment. It is absolutely necessary, in order to create inclusive development, to work toward gender equality in areas such as education and the workforce.

Towards a Brighter Future: Empowerment via Education and the Development of Skills

1. **Education That Is Open To All**

   It is imperative that inclusive education methods be encouraged in order to guarantee that people from all walks of life have access to educational opportunities of a high standard. This includes making accommodations for students who have impairments, offering linguistic support for students who do not speak English as their first language, and eliminating barriers to education for members of underrepresented communities.

2. **Curriculum that is pertinent**

   The educational curricula need to be revised so that they are more in line with the shifting requirements of the labor market. Students are better prepared to meet the demands of today's workforce when the curriculum includes both hands-on skills and digital literacy training in addition to critical thinking activities. To ensure that educational programs are relevant to the needs of the working world, educational institutions should collaborate with various industries.

3. **Initiatives for Continuing Education and Training**

   It is crucial to promote efforts for lifelong learning in order to provide individuals with the skills necessary for the adaptation of their careers and for their own personal progress. These initiatives may take the shape of online courses, programs that provide vocational training, or flexible educational pathways that are geared toward students of varying ages.

4. **The promotion of gender equality and inclusiveness**

The prioritization of efforts should be placed on promoting gender equality and inclusivity in educational and professional development settings. This involves the elimination of discrimination on the basis of gender, the provision of support for female students who are pursuing degrees in STEM subjects, and the creation of an atmosphere that enables women to pursue professions and leadership roles in all fields.

Education and skill development are tremendous forces that propel individuals as well as societies forward. They are the engines that power economic growth, social mobility, and international competitiveness.

Education helps people grow their cognitive, social, and emotional intelligence, while the development of skills improves employability, professional advancement, and innovative thinking. In order to build a learning ecosystem that is more welcoming and equitable for marginalized groups, it is necessary to address problems such as unequal access to resources, mismatched skill sets, and gender discrepancies.

The way forward requires a commitment to gender equality, as well as inclusive education, relevant curricula, and efforts for learning that continues throughout life. Education and skill development should be prioritized because they allow individuals and societies to reach their greatest potential, which in turn fosters empowerment and prosperity for everyone. Education and the cultivation of relevant skills are the linchpins upon which a more promising and equitable future can be built for individuals and communities all around the world.

8.3 Charitable Giving and Philanthropy

Philanthropy and charitable giving have been important forces behind positive change all across the world for a very long time. The giving of one's time, resources, and financial assistance on a voluntarily basis in order to aid a variety of causes and work toward the resolution of urgent social, environmental, and humanitarian problems is included in these practices. The influence of charity giving and philanthropy extends far beyond monetary contributions. It encompasses a wide range of activities and ways that provide a significant ripple effect in society. In the course of this investigation, we will investigate the significance of charity giving and philanthropy by investigating the role that these activities play in generating innovation, increasing social well-being, and tackling global concerns. The importance of openness, accountability, and strategic giving will be emphasized as we continue our discussion of these practices, during which we will also investigate the difficulties and opportunities that are linked with them.

The Importance of Donating to Charities and Engaging in Philanthropy

1. **The Welfare of Society and the Strengthening of Communities**
   Donations to charitable organizations and other forms of philanthropy play an essential part in advancing community empowerment and social well-being. Philanthropic activities assist improve the quality of life for vulnerable populations by providing financial support for critical services such as education, healthcare, and social welfare programs. This, in turn, contributes to the development of a sense of community togetherness.

2. **Finding Solutions to Worldwide Problems**
   Donations to charities and other forms of philanthropy are absolutely necessary in order to effectively address urgent problems on a global scale, such as inequality in healthcare and the effects of climate change.
   Research, advocacy, and the development of creative solutions are all areas that get funding from charitable foundations, organizations, and individuals in order to address the complexities of these problems.

3. **Fostering Creativity and Scientific Investigation**
   Philanthropy acts as a driving force behind technological advancement and scientific investigation. It offers financial support for the pursuit of scientific and technological advances, as well as innovative approaches to resolving existing issues. Research in fields such as healthcare, renewable energy, and social entrepreneurship is frequently supported by donors, which helps to stimulate both development and discovery in these fields.

4. **Increasing Our Community's Impact**

Through strategic giving and collaborative efforts, charitable organizations and individuals alike have the ability to magnify the positive effects of their work on the world. They are able to make use of the resources and networks available to them to solve systemic difficulties, affect changes in policy, and promote projects that are beneficial to a diverse range of members of society.

Methods and Procedures Regarding Charitable Giving

1. **Funds that are Advised by Donors**
   Donor-advised funds are a popular type of philanthropic vehicle because they enable individuals, families, and companies to make tax-deductible contributions to a fund, advise on how to distribute the contributions to charitable organizations, and grow the assets tax-free over the course of time. This makes donor-advised funds an attractive option for charitable giving. Donors have

more flexibility and influence over the strategic direction of their donations thanks to this strategy.

2. **Investing with an Impact**

effect investing is a form of investing that seeks to maximize both financial returns and positive social and environmental effect. While looking for a financial return, investors put their money into enterprises, projects, and funds that have a good social or environmental impact on the world. Impact investment is an effective strategy for addressing global concerns while also preserving financial viability.

3. **Responsible Corporate Citizenship, Also Known as CSR**

In order to contribute something back to the communities that they are responsible for, corporate entities frequently participate in corporate social responsibility (CSR) activities. CSR refers to activities such as monetary donations, staff volunteer programs, and sustainability initiatives that are in line with the ideals of a company and are of benefit to society.

4. **Leave a Gift in Your Will**

Donating one's assets or financial resources to charity organizations after one's death is an act that is referred to as legacy giving or planned giving. This type of giving requires setting provisions in one's estate plan to accomplish this goal. This strategy enables individuals to create a legacy that will endure while also contributing to issues that are meaningful to them.

Philanthropy and Other Forms of Charitable Giving Present Both Obstacles and Opportunities

1. **Responsibility and openness to the public**

Giving to charity and engaging in philanthropy present a number of issues, one of which is maintaining accountability and openness. In order to foster confidence and credibility, philanthropic foundations, charitable organizations, and donors all need to maintain transparency in their operations, financial reporting, and effect assessments.

2. **The Efficient Distribution of Resources**

For philanthropy and charitable giving to have the greatest possible impact, it is essential to allocate resources strategically. Donors and organizations ought to do exhaustive due diligence, evaluate the efficacy of programs, and make certain that resources are channeled toward efforts that have the most potential to bring about positive change.

3. **Working Together and Coordinating Efforts**

It is necessary for philanthropic organizations to work together and coordinate their efforts in order to effectively solve complicated global concerns. Philanthropic groups can increase their effect and accomplish more meaningful achievements by collaborating with one another to pool their resources, skills, and networks.

4. **Generosity that won't go to waste**

Philanthropy places a significant emphasis on the concept of long-term viability. It is absolutely necessary, in order to solve continuous problems such as poverty, environmental preservation, and public health, to make certain that charitable activities can be maintained throughout the course of a lengthy period of time. This may involve long-term commitments to various causes, as well as the establishment of endowment funds and grant-making techniques.

Philanthropy that is both strategic and impactful is the way forward.

1. **Making decisions based on the analysis of data**
   The use of data to inform decisions is an essential component of effective philanthropy. Donors and organizations should use data and evidence-based methodologies to evaluate the efficacy of their initiatives, measure the impact of those initiatives, and adapt their tactics in accordance with the findings of these evaluations.

2. **Working Together and Forming Partnerships**
   It is impossible to effectively solve complicated problems without the cooperation and engagement of several philanthropic organizations. In order to have a greater collective influence, philanthropic organizations and foundations, as well as other types of nonprofits, should collaborate, exchange information, and combine their respective resources.

3. **Long-term viability**
   The concept of long-term viability ought to be at the center of all charitable giving. Philanthropic organizations should guarantee that their work contributes to the well-being of future generations, encourage ecologically responsible methods, and evaluate the long-term viability of the initiatives they undertake.

4. **Embracing Difference and Fostering Inclusion**

Philanthropy is an area that ought to make inclusivity and diversity its top priorities. It is the responsibility of charitable organizations to ensure that their leadership, decision-making processes, and projects reflect the varied voices and points of view of the communities they seek to serve.

Donations to charities and other forms of philanthropy have the ability to bring about positive change, find solutions to global problems, and improve the well-being of society. These strategies help to maintain critical services, encourage innovation, and provide communities with increased agency. It is absolutely necessary to employ strategic approaches that place a strong emphasis on responsibility, collaboration, sustainability, and inclusion in order to successfully manage the hurdles and grab the opportunities that exist in the philanthropic sector.

Donors, charitable organizations, and philanthropic foundations that are dedicated to making a positive impact on the world hold the key to philanthropy's bright future. Philanthropy has the potential to continue to be a driving force behind positive change all around the world if organizations engage in the practice of aligning their efforts with the most pressing global challenges, making decisions based on evidence, and embracing sustainability.

8.4 Trading's Contribution to Sustainable Development Goals

Trading, which is a key driver of economic growth and globalization, plays an important role in the advancement of the Sustainable Development Goals (SDGs) that have been established by the United Nations. The Sustainable Development Goals (SDGs) aim to address a wide variety of global issues, ranging from the elimination of poverty and hunger to the promotion of environmental preservation and social equality. Trading operations, when carried out in a responsible and environmentally conscious manner, have the potential to make significant contributions toward the accomplishment of these goals. During this in-depth investigation, we will delve into the complex relationship that exists between sustainable development and trading. Specifically, we will investigate the ways in which trading encourages economic expansion, advances social welfare, and finds solutions to environmental problems. In addition to this, we will discuss the obstacles that must be overcome as well as the opportunities that can be taken advantage of in order to achieve the Sustainable Development Goals (SDGs), with an emphasis on the significance of inclusion, ethical behaviors, and innovation.

The Role of Commercial Activity in the Expansion of the Economy

1. **The Elimination of Poverty**

   Trading carries with it the possibility of rescuing people as well as entire communities from impoverishment. Trading activities have the potential to accelerate economic growth in developing nations, boost income levels, and reduce poverty rates. These benefits can be achieved because trading operations provide access to worldwide markets and create economic opportunities.

2. **The Generation of Jobs**

   The generation of jobs is aided by commerce, particularly in sectors of the economy that are dependent on exports and imports. Expanded trade is beneficial to the manufacturing, agricultural, and service sectors because it creates employment possibilities and increases labor force participation, ultimately helping to the achievement of Sustainable Development Goal 8 (Decent Work and Economic Growth).

3. **The Building of New Infrastructure**

Increasing investments in infrastructure are frequently the result of economic expansion that is driven by commercial trading activity. Advancing Sustainable Development Goal 9 (which focuses on Industry, Innovation, and Infrastructure) and facilitating commerce requires the establishment of transportation networks, ports, and logistics hubs.

The Contribution of Trading to the Welfare of Society

1. **Availability of Educational and Medical Facilities**
   The expansion of trade can lead to higher levels of government revenues and public spending, which in turn can enable greater access to education and healthcare services. Both Goal 4 (Quality Education) and Goal 3 (Good Health and Well-being) stand to gain from the resources made available as a result of growth associated to trade.
2. **Parity between the sexes**
   Trading goods and services can have a beneficial effect on gender equality if it creates more chances for women to participate in the labor force and increases the economic autonomy of women. The achievement of gender equality, which is the goal of Sustainable Development Goal 5, is compatible with economic growth caused by trading activity.
3. **A decrease in levels of inequality**

Increased economic activity connected with trading can assist reduce income inequality by providing chances for underserved groups to engage in the global economy. This makes a contribution to Sustainable Development Goal 10 (Reduced Inequality), which is one of the 17 Sustainable Development Goals.

The Role That Trading Plays in Ensuring the Sustainability of the Environment

1. **Eco-Friendly Business Procedures**
   Green trade practices have the potential to promote eco-friendly and responsible trade since they focus sustainability and environmental responsibility. Both Sustainable Development Goal 12 (Responsible Consumption and Production) and Sustainable Development Goal 13 (Climate Action) are aligned with sustainable trade practices.
2. **Agriculture that is sustainable and the use of renewable energy**
   The promotion of Sustainable Development Goal 7 (Affordable and Clean Energy) and Sustainable Development Goal 2 (Zero Hunger) can be helped along by the development and spread of renewable energy technologies and sustainable agriculture practices.
3. **Preserving the Earth's Flora and Fauna**

Trading can be used as a strategy for conservation if it contributes to the fight against illicit wildlife trade and the promotion of sustainable resource management, which is part of Sustainable Development Goal 15 (Life on Land).

Incorporating Trading into the Sustainable Development Goals: Obstacles and Opportunities

1. **Methods That Are Both Ethical And Sustainable**
   The requirement for trading practices that are both ethical and sustainable is one of the obstacles that must be overcome in order to harness trade for the Sustainable Development Goals (SDGs). In order to accomplish the Sustainable Development Goals (SDGs), it is essential to ensure that commerce is carried out in a manner that is responsible and that respects labor rights, environmental protection, and human rights.

2. **Openness to All and Ethical Business Practices**
   To ensure that the benefits of various economic operations are distributed fairly, inclusivity and fair trade are two of the most important factors to consider. It is absolutely necessary to take steps to increase the participation of small and medium-sized businesses (SMEs) and underserved communities in the international trading system.

3. **The Building of New Infrastructure**
   The development of infrastructure is a critical factor in facilitating trade; nevertheless, it may also provide environmental and social issues. It is a challenging task to strike a balance between the need for effective transportation and logistics and the preservation of the environment.

4. **Legal and Regulatory Structures**

It is a difficult undertaking to develop and harmonize international regulatory frameworks that support the Sustainable Development Goals (SDGs) and promote responsible trade. It is necessary to make sure that sustainable development is prioritized in all trade agreements and regulations.

The Way Forward: Sustainable Business Practices in Support of the Sustainable Development Goals

1. **Eco-Friendly Procurement and Distribution Channels**
   It is of the utmost importance to promote the implementation of ethical supply chains and sustainable sourcing practices. The reduction of waste, the promotion of fair labor practices, and the prioritization of ecologically responsible production should be the focus of businesses and other commercial entities.

2. **Economic Strategies That Include All Parties**
   It is imperative that national governments and international organizations give top priority to the development of inclusive trade policies. These policies should

encourage the participation of small and medium-sized businesses (SMEs), firms owned by women, and disadvantaged communities in global trade. The formation of trade agreements should prioritize the promotion of equitable access to global markets.

3. **Innovation and technological advancement**
Utilizing new technologies and innovative processes can improve the trading industry's long-term viability and overall efficiency. Transparency and traceability in supply chains can be supported by digital solutions, blockchain technology, and data analytics, which can help promote responsible business practices.

4. **Working Together and Forming Partnerships**

For the Sustainable Development Goals (SDGs) to be reached through commercial endeavors, it is necessary for governments, private businesses, civil societies, and international organizations to work together and form partnerships. Stakeholders can more effectively align their efforts and resources to collectively address global challenges if they collaborate and work together.

Trading is an important contributor to the United Nations' Sustainable Development Goals since it is a powerful engine of economic growth, social well-being, and environmental sustainability. Trading operations can have a positive impact on a number of Sustainable Development Goals (SDGs) by increasing economic prosperity, increasing access to education and healthcare, and developing sustainable behaviors.

To guarantee that trading effectively contributes to the Sustainable Development Goals (SDGs),

it is necessary to address challenges such as ethical issues, inclusion, and the requirement for sustainable practices. The international community has the ability to harness the full potential of trading in order to advance the Sustainable Development Goals (SDGs) and build a society that is more equal and affluent if they adopt sustainable and inclusive trading practices, encourage responsible sourcing, and leverage technology and innovation.

Chapter 9

Future Trends and Prospects

The course of the future is going to be determined by a wide variety of shifting elements, including developments in technology, shifts in the economy, sociological transitions, and environmental issues. Predicting and preparing for what lies ahead is a difficult undertaking that requires an analysis of emerging trends, potential opportunities, and the uncertainties that will influence our world in the future years. Predicting and preparing for what lies ahead is a complex endeavor that involves a study of emerging trends, potential opportunities, and the uncertainties. The purpose of this investigation is to present a complete summary of future tendencies and prospects across a variety of fields, including as technology, economics, society, and the environment. By analyzing these trends, we may acquire understanding into the ways in which they may affect our lives and the way that the future will unfold.

Recent Technological Developments and the Emergence of the Digital Age

1. **Machine Learning and Artificial Intelligence (also known as AI)**
   Numerous sectors are on the cusp of seeing a sea change as a direct result of the rapid development of AI and machine learning. Automation driven by artificial intelligence, predictive analytics, and natural language processing are all reshaping how organizations function and the kind of services they provide to customers. The possibility of computers that can teach themselves and algorithms with artificial intelligence is altering many different industries, including healthcare and finance.

2. **Computing on the Quantum Level**
   The unrivaled processing capacity of quantum computing has the potential to usher in a paradigm shift across a variety of industries, including encryption, the search for new drugs, and materials science. Despite the fact that they are still in their infancy, quantum computers present the possibility of finding solutions to difficult problems that are currently beyond the capacity of classical computers.

3. **The Internet of Things (IoT)**

   The Internet of Things is expected to continue its rapid expansion, linking even more traditional systems and equipment to the web.

   This trend brings opportunities for enhanced efficiency, sustainability, and convenience; but, it also raises worries about the environmental impact of an increasing number of connected devices as well as data security and privacy issues.

4. **Technology Based on 5G**

   The broad use of 5G technology has the potential to improve connection by lowering latency, allowing for quicker data transmission, and opening the door to the creation of novel applications such as augmented reality and driverless vehicles.

5. **Genetic engineering and other forms of biotechnology**

Breakthroughs in medicine, tailored treatment, and increased crop yields are all possible outcomes that could be brought about by developments in biotechnology and genetic engineering. However, these advances also present issues in terms of ethics and regulatory oversight.

Economic Tendencies and the Shifting Global Landscape

1. **The Digital Economy and Online Shopping**

   The growth of the digital economy, which is exemplified by e-commerce, the provision of services online, and the gig economy, is continuing. This development presents chances for new kinds of businesses, as well as for working from home and gaining access to international markets.

2. **Environmental Responsibility and a Greener Economy**

   The shift toward a green economy, which is being pushed by concerns about climate change, presents opportunities for environmentally friendly technologies, renewable energy, and sustainable agriculture. The concept of sustainability as a growth driver is gaining more and more attention from governments, businesses, and investors.

3. **Disparities and Inequality in the Economic System**

   In many regions of the world, economic inequality is a critical matter that needs immediate attention. In order to address these inequalities, concerted efforts need to be made, and policies need to be revised, in order to promote more fair access to opportunities and resources.

4. **The Impact of Technology on Working Conditions**

   The labor market is undergoing significant change as a result of automation and AI.

   There is a possibility that certain jobs will go extinct; nevertheless, new opportunities are opening up in a variety of disciplines, including robotics, data analytics, and digital marketing. The task of properly preparing the labor force for this transition is an essential one.

5. **Changes in the Geopolitical Landscape Caused by International Trade**

As a result of shifting political dynamics, tariffs, and trade agreements, the global trading landscape is currently going through a period of transition. The future of international collaboration, the reconfiguration of supply chains, and economic diplomacy will all have an impact on the economy of the entire world.

Alterations in Social Structure and Cultural Practices

1. **Shifts in the Country's Population**

   Changes in population demographics, such as growing urbanization and an aging population, are driving these societal shifts. The potential include changes in consumer behavior as well as issues in the healthcare industry and opportunities in urban development.

2. **Education and further education throughout a lifetime**

   The need for ongoing education and the improvement of skills is becoming increasingly prevalent. For individuals to maintain their level of competitiveness in the job market, the possibility of learning throughout one's entire life as well as the requirement for education systems that are flexible are becoming increasingly vital.

3. **Acceptance of Differences and Participation**

   The expectations of society with regard to diversity and inclusion are always shifting. The social fabric of communities and organizations will be shaped according to the prospects for equality and social justice, as well as the acceptance of varied points of view.

4. **Psychological health and overall well-being**

   The importance of maintaining one's mental health is increasingly being recognized. The future holds the potential for increased knowledge of mental health issues, the removal of the associated stigma, and the incorporation of mental well-being into healthcare and workplace policy.

5. **Urbanization and technologically advanced cities**

The current trends in urbanization are presenting potential opportunities for the creation of smart cities. These cities have the potential to improve urban planning, increase the efficiency of transportation, and provide a higher quality of life for the people who live there.

Environmental Difficulties and the Question of Sustainability

1. **The Changing Climate and Its Effects and Adaptation**

   The difficulties brought on by climate change are getting harder to deal with. In order to ensure a sustainable future, it is essential to investigate potential means of mitigation, such as renewable energy and carbon capture technologies, as well as the necessity of developing adaption methods to deal with extreme weather occurrences.

2. **The protection of biological diversity**
   The alarming rate at which biodiversity is being lost is one of the most important environmental concerns. Restoring habitats, protecting wildlife, and engaging in environmentally responsible land use are all potential avenues for the conservation of biodiversity.

3. **Waste Reduction and the Transition to a Circular Economy**
   The shift toward a circular economy presents opportunities to cut down on waste and increase the effectiveness with which resources are used. This covers activities such as recycling, reuse, and lowering the products' overall impact on the environment.

4. **The Scarcity of Water and the Implications for Sustainable Management**
   In many parts of the world, the availability of fresh water is becoming increasingly limited. Prospects for sustainable water management and conservation include the development of improved water infrastructure, the implementation of more productive agricultural practices, and the exercise of responsible consumption.

5. **Innovative Technical Answers to Environmental Problems**

There is hope for resolving environmental issues and moving to a more sustainable future thanks to developments in technology. Some examples of these developments are solar electricity, electric vehicles, and sustainable agricultural practices.
Both difficulties and prospects are involved.

1. **Concerns Regarding Ethics and Personal Privacy**
   Concerns are raised regarding genetic alteration, data privacy, and algorithmic bias as a result of the ethical implications of technology, notably artificial intelligence and biotechnology. The creation of ethical principles, the establishment of regulation, and the responsible application of these technologies are all possibilities.

2. **Preparing for pandemics and global health concerns**
   The COVID-19 pandemic brought to light the significance of global health and the relevance of being prepared for pandemics. Possible outcomes include more money being invested in hospital facilities, research on vaccines, and enhanced international collaboration.

3. **Education and the Promotion of Competencies**
   It is a huge obstacle to face to ensure that individuals have access to high-quality educational and professional development opportunities. Opportunities

include cutting-edge online learning platforms, attempts to bridge the digital divide, and vocational training programs.

4. **Conflicts on the Geopolitical Stage and International Collaboration**
Global stability is being threatened by a number of factors, including geopolitical tensions and shifting patterns in international relations. The prospects for diplomacy, the resolution of conflicts, and increased cooperation are crucial to the achievement of world peace in the future.

5. **Management of Resources in a Sustainable Manner**

The obstacle of environmentally responsible resource management is absolutely necessary for the protection of the natural world. There is potential for progress in the form of international agreements, technical advances, and public awareness campaigns to encourage the responsible use of resources.

The Next Steps: Finding Your Way Through Uncertainty

1. **Working Together and Using Methods From Several Disciplines**
It is essential for governments, companies, academic institutions, and members of civil society to work together in order to effectively address complex problems. Multidisciplinary techniques that make use of a wide variety of knowledge have the potential to result in the development of novel solutions.

2. **Capacity for Adaptation and Resilience**
It is extremely important to work on building resiliency and adaptation on an individual, community, and organizational level. A proactive approach is one that involves making preparations for unanticipated interruptions and uncertainty.

3. **Practices that are innovative and environmentally friendly**
Across order to help address global concerns, it is possible to promote innovation and the adoption of sustainable practices across a variety of industries, including technology and agriculture, as well as healthcare and energy.

4. **Education and Continued Professional Development**
Putting an emphasis on education and continuing one's education throughout one's life is absolutely necessary in order to provide individuals with the competencies and information they need to successfully navigate a world that is always evolving.

5. **Considerations of an Ethical Nature**

To address ethical concerns, such as data privacy and genetic engineering, continuous debate, regulation, and responsible behaviors are required in order to guarantee that technological advancements will be beneficial to society without causing it any harm.

The future is going to be characterized by a patchwork of different trends, problems, and opportunities that will determine the course that our planet takes. We can navigate the route forward with resiliency, inventiveness, and a dedication to create a more sustainable, fair, and prosperous future for generations to come if we grasp these dynamics and proactively address them. In spite of the fact that there are a great deal of unknowns, our ability to adjust, work together, and make well-informed decisions will serve as our compass as we navigate the shifting terrain of the future.

9.1 Emerging Market Opportunities

Emerging markets are regions of the world that are experiencing significant economic growth and development. These regions are typically distinguished by a growing middle class, increased urbanization, and expanding consumer marketplaces. Businesses, investors, and governments that are looking to tap into new growth areas can find significant opportunity in these regions. During this in-depth investigation, we are going to look into the notion of emerging markets, identify major possibilities that exist within these markets, analyze the obstacles that they bring, and think about the strategies that are required to leverage the potential for growth in these areas.

Acquiring Knowledge about Emerging Markets

Growth of the Economy: In comparison to more developed economies, emerging countries typically display faster rates of economic expansion. This expansion is being driven by a variety of factors, including industrialization, urbanization, and an increasing labor force.

Alterations in Demographics A large number of developing countries have populations that are young and on the rise. This demographic dividend has the potential to stimulate higher levels of consumption, innovation, and overall productivity.

Emerging markets typically display characteristics associated with urbanization, such as a considerable population migration from rural to urban areas. Opportunities arise in many different industries as a result of urbanization, including the housing, infrastructure, transportation, and service sectors.

Increasing Numbers of People in the Middle Many emerging markets are characterized by the growth of their middle classes. When people's salaries go up, so does their capacity for consumption, which drives up the demand for a wide variety of different products and services.

Natural Resources: Emerging markets frequently hold valuable natural resources, which can be both a source of economic growth and a difficulty, as they can lead to resource-related disputes. Emerging markets' possession of these valuable natural resources can be both a source of economic growth and a challenge.

Emerging markets are becoming increasingly connected into the global economy, which enables enterprises to extend their operations and tap into new consumer bases. This phenomenon is referred to as globalization.

Investment and Business Opportunity Resulting from Need for Improved Infrastructure The need for improved infrastructure, including transportation, energy, and communication networks, results in business and investment opportunities.

Possibilities available in newly developing markets

1. **Markets for Consumer Goods**
   Middle classes in emerging nations are expanding rapidly and gaining greater purchasing power as a result.
   This opens up a lot of doors for companies in the retail, consumer goods, and online shopping industries, among others. Growth that is substantial can result from adapting one's goods and services to the preferences and prerequisites of one's target markets.

2. **Services in the Financial Sector**
   There is a large amount of untapped expansion potential in the emerging market finance sector. This encompasses financial services such as banking and insurance, as well as technology and microfinance. Opportunities for investment and wealth management are growing along with the number of people who have access to various financial services.

3. **Energies renouvelables**
   Several growing markets are looking for environmentally friendly alternatives to satisfy their demands for energy. Opportunities exist in the green energy industry for investors and businesses to participate in renewable energy projects such as solar, wind, and hydropower generation.

4. **Agricultural and Agricultural-Related Businesses**
   Agriculture serves as a vital support system for a significant number of developing economies. Opportunities can be found in enhancing agricultural practices, strengthening food supply chains, and fostering the growth of agribusiness enterprises that serve customers in both the domestic and international markets.

5. **Health and Welfare**
   The expansion of the middle class in emerging nations is the primary factor behind the rise in demand for medical care services. This covers medical facilities such as hospitals and clinics, as well as telemedicine, drugs, and medical equipment.

6. **Online business and technological advancements**
   The digital revolution is penetrating emerging nations, which is offering opportunities in a variety of industries including mobile technology, e-commerce platforms, and digital payment systems. The use of smartphones is gradually becoming more widespread, which improves both connectivity and access to markets.

7. **The Construction of New Facilities**
   In a good number of emerging markets, there is a large demand for the construction of infrastructure. This involves the establishment of networks for transportation, the generation and distribution of energy, the transmission of information, and the development of real estate. Putting in place new infrastructure typically requires partnerships and investments over a protracted period of time.

8. **Instructional**

The number of students who require educational services is expected to increase in emerging markets. Because of this, there are chances available for vocational training programs, educational institutions, and online learning platforms.

Emerging Markets Present a Number of Obstacles and Dangers

1. **Risks Associated with Politics and Regulation**
   The political environments in emerging markets are often fragile, and they see frequent regulatory shifts. Investors have a responsibility to navigate these uncertainties, which may have an effect on the operations of businesses and their profits.

2. **The Unpredictability of Currencies and Exchange Rates**
   Businesses that operate in emerging economies may experience disruptions to their financial
   stability as a result of currency devaluation and volatility in exchange rates. Hedging and diversifying currency exposure are two strategies that can be used to reduce the impact of these risks.

3. **Deficits in the Infrastructure**
   Both the functioning of businesses and the expansion of the economy can be hampered by insufficient levels of infrastructure. Examples of this include inadequate transportation and energy supplies. To fill these voids, businesses could have to make investments in infrastructure or collaborate with government agencies.

4. **Bribery and inefficiency in public administration**
   In emerging markets, problems such as bureaucratic red tape and corrupt officials are frequently highlighted as obstacles. To successfully navigate these challenges, you may need to implement stringent compliance controls and increase transparency throughout your business operations.

5. **Variations in Sociocultural Practices**
   Because of these cultural differences and variations in consumer tastes, it may be necessary for firms to modify their products, marketing techniques, and business structures so that they are appropriate for the local environment.

6. **Dangers to the Economy and the Finances**
   Emerging markets are often more vulnerable to economic downturns and financial crises than developed ones are. Businesses have a responsibility to evaluate the robustness of the regional financial system and make contingency plans for potential economic disruptions.

7. **Dangers Associated with the Law and Intellectual Property**

There is a possibility that legal and intellectual property protection will be weaker in certain emerging markets. It is absolutely necessary for businesses operating in these locations to take steps to safeguard their intellectual property and successfully navigate the local legal systems.

Strategies for Capitalizing on the Opportunities Offered by Emerging Markets

1. **Meticulous Investigation of the Market**
   Carry out exhaustive research into the market in order to gain an understanding of the local environment, consumer behavior, competition, and regulatory environment. This information can help businesses make decisions and formulate plans for entering new markets.

2. **Partnerships in the Community**
   Developing strategic alliances with local businesses or groups can provide invaluable market intelligence and networking opportunities. Local partners can also assist in navigating the hurdles posed by regulatory authorities and the cultural gaps that exist.

3. **Measures to Reduce the Danger**
   It is important to put in place mechanisms for mitigating risk, such as currency hedging, political risk insurance, and legal safeguards. Spread your business operations over a number of different markets to decrease your vulnerability to the dangers of any one market.

4. **Environmental Stewardship and the Responsibility of Businesses**
   Adopt methods of corporate responsibility and sustainability that are in line with the principles and requirements of the local community. This has the potential to improve the company's reputation and cultivate positive relationships with the areas in which it operates.

5. **Perspective on the Long Term**
   When dealing with emerging markets, it is important to think in the long run. There is the potential for profits in the short term, but in order to achieve long-term success, patience, effort, and dedication to the market are typically required.

6. **The cultivation of talent**
   Make an investment in the cultivation of talent as well as training in order to build a skilled local workforce. This not only helps the operations of the business, but it also makes a contribution to the growth of the community in which the firm is located.

7. **Interaction with the Government**

Engage with the local governments in order to comprehend the goals they have set for themselves and investigate the possibilities of public-private partnerships. The compliance with regulations and the development of infrastructure can both be made easier by collaboration with government agencies.

There are considerable prospects for expansion across a variety of industries that can be found in emerging economies, including healthcare, technology, consumer goods, and infrastructure markets. To successfully navigate these markets, however, demands a deep comprehension of the specific difficulties and dangers that they present.

The full potential of developing markets can be unlocked for businesses and investors who approach these growing regions with a strategic, long-term view as well as a dedication to ethical and environmentally sustainable business practices. They may contribute to the growth of the economy, the creation of new jobs, and an improvement in living standards in emerging countries while simultaneously accomplishing their own business goals if they take advantage of the opportunities and aggressively address the problems.

9.2 Integration with E-commerce and Digital Payments

The purchasing and selling of products and services over the internet is referred to as "e-commerce," which is short for "electronic commerce." The past few years have seen an exponential boom in e-commerce, which has fundamentally altered the shopping habits of consumers as well as the operations of businesses. The implementation of digital payment methods, which ushered in a sea change in the way business is done, is one of the most important aspects of this transformation. During this in-depth investigation, we will delve into the realm of e-commerce and digital payments, addressing their interdependence as well as the benefits, problems, and the revolutionary power that they hold in the contemporary landscape of business.

The Emergence of the E-commerce Revolution

1. **Easily accessed and a convenient location**

   E-commerce empowers customers to complete purchases from the convenience of their own homes or from any location with access to the internet. Due to the fact that it is so convenient, many people now choose it above other options, particularly in situations when there is a limitation on either the amount of time available or the physical closeness to stores.

2. **Impact on the World**

   The elimination of geographical limitations made possible by online platforms paves the way for businesses to communicate with customers all over the world. This increased market reach is especially helpful for small and medium-sized businesses (SMEs) that are working to broaden their consumer base.

3. **Accessibility Around the Clock**

   Customers have the convenience of shopping at any time of day or night thanks to the availability of e-commerce websites and platforms, which are open around the clock. This characteristic is especially enticing in a world in which conventional shops with brick-and-mortar locations keep regular business hours.

4. **A Wide Variety of Products to Choose From**

   E-commerce platforms provide access to a vast assortment of goods and services, frequently exceeding what is available in a conventional store's physical space. Consumers have access to a diversified marketplace, which enables them to find products that are exclusive to a certain niche market.

5. **A Comparison of Prices**

Consumers have the capacity to make informed decisions when they are able to compare costs across a variety of websites, which helps to ensure that they get good value for the money they spend.

The Importance of Electronic Payments

1. **Credit Cards, Debit Cards, and ATMs**

   The use of credit cards and debit cards for internet transactions is extremely common.

   Convenience, safety, and adaptability are some of the benefits that they provide to customers and companies alike. Payment gateways are the normal processing mechanism for card payments, which ensures the safety of financial transactions conducted online.

2. **Wallets for mobile devices**

   Mobile wallets, such as Apple Pay, Google Pay, and Samsung Pay, allow users to save payment information on their smartphones and make contactless purchases in brick-and-mortar stores as well as online. Mobile wallets are becoming increasingly popular. They are becoming increasingly common since they are so simple to employ.

3. **Using the Bank's Website**

   Customers now have the ability to move money directly from their bank accounts to e-commerce platforms thanks to online banking. The utilization of bank transfers and payments processed through an automated clearinghouse (ACH) is a standard practice for online transactions.

4. **Virtual currency or cryptographic money**

   Cryptocurrencies, such as Bitcoin and Ethereum, are examples of digital or virtual currencies that offer a method of conducting transactions online that is both secure and decentralized. They are gaining an increasing level of acceptance among companies operating in the e-commerce market.

5. **Electronic wallets**

E-wallets, such as PayPal and Skrill, give customers the ability to securely store monies and conduct online transactions without exposing their financial information. They are especially common in international e-commerce and the conduct of transactions across international borders.

The Advantages That Come With Combining E-commerce With Digital Payments

1. **The ease of use**
   The convenience provided by the combination of online shopping and digital payment methods is unmatched. Customers no longer have to physically go to stores to make purchases because they can do so from their mobile devices with just a few clicks.
2. **Safekeeping**
   In many cases, traditional payment methods are less safe than digital payment methods. Protecting sensitive financial information with encryption and authentication processes helps to lower the likelihood of fraudulent activity and other types of unapproved activities.
3. **Velocity**
   When compared to traditional methods of payment, digital payment processing is significantly quicker. Instantaneous receipt of payment confirmations guarantees a streamlined and productive buying experience.
4. **Efficient Use of Resources**
   When compared to traditional payment methods for businesses, such as the processing of checks or the handling of cash, digital payments, such as those made with a credit card, can be more cost effective. Additionally, the overhead costs that are associated with traditional retailers can be reduced through the use of online shopping.
5. **Impact on the World**
   E-commerce and online payment methods make it possible for enterprises to reach customers all over the world. This opens up more opportunities in the market and could lead to an increase in revenue.
6. **Data Insights**

E-commerce platforms have the ability to acquire significant data on the preferences and behaviors of customers. Analyzing this data allows for the improvement of marketing strategies, the personalization of shopping experiences, and the enhancement of product offerings.

Concerns and Things to Take Into Account

1. **Concerns Regarding Safety**
   Concerns over the safety of digital payments have been raised as a result of the proliferation of cyberattacks and data breaches. To ensure the safety of their customers' information, businesses need to make significant investments in sophisticated cybersecurity solutions.

2. **Fraudulent Payments**

   There are numerous types of fraudulent activity that can occur with digital payments, including chargebacks and identity theft. For e-commerce enterprises to succeed, fraud protection measures that actually work need to be implemented.

3. **Observance of All Regulations**

   Companies that deal in e-commerce have to negotiate a complicated regulatory environment and fulfill stringent compliance requirements. This covers legislation pertaining to taxes and foreign trade, as well as laws protecting personal data.

4. **Availability of Access**

   There is a segment of the population that does not have access to digital payment options like credit cards or cellphones. To appeal to a wider range of customers, online retailers should give careful consideration to the diversity of the payment methods they offer.

5. **The Trust of the Customers**

Establishing and upholding trust is of the utmost importance in online business. Customers have a right to be confidence that their personal and financial information is safeguarded, and businesses have a responsibility to ensure this.

The Power to Make Things Different

The convergence of online shopping and electronic payment methods is causing a multifaceted shift in the competitive environment of business.

1. **The Transformation of Conventional Shopping**

   The traditional retail industry has been shaken up by the rise of e-commerce since internet buying platforms provide an alternative that is frequently more convenient than traditional shopping methods. Traditional retailers have been compelled to adjust their business models in order to accommodate shifting customer demands.

2. **The growth of small and medium-sized businesses (also known as SMEs)**

   E-commerce has made it easier for small and medium-sized businesses (SMEs) to enter global markets and compete with larger corporations. The utilization of e-commerce platforms has resulted in tremendous expansion for a great number of smaller firms.

3. **Customization of experience**

   The purchasing experience can be made more personalized through the use of data analytics and artificial intelligence on e-commerce platforms. This involves making individualized suggestions for products, tailoring marketing messaging to individual customers, and running personalized promotions.

4. **Commerce Across National Borders**

   Consumers are now able to acquire goods from overseas vendors as a result of the proliferation of digital payment methods, which has made possible cross-border e-commerce. This has resulted in expanded options for customers and new market opportunities for enterprises.

5. **Innovation as well as progress made in technological areas**

Both the online retail and online payment industries are hives of creative activity. The sector is continually being reshaped by emerging technologies, such as augmented reality for simulating shopping experiences and blockchain for ensuring the security of financial transactions.

Tendencies and Prospects for the Future

1. **The Mobile Commerce (often abbreviated as M-commerce)**
   It is anticipated that growth in mobile commerce will occur in tandem with the proliferation of smartphone use. The primary focus of companies will shift to the adaptation of their online storefronts to mobile platforms and the creation of mobile payment systems.

2. **Payments using contactless technology**
   The use of contactless payment technologies such as NFC (Near Field Communication) and QR codes is becoming increasingly commonplace. This trend is being driven by people's demand for transactions that are both touchless and convenient.

3. **International online business transactions**
   It is anticipated that growth in international online trade will continue, which will present companies with new options to access foreign markets. In order to cater to a wide variety of audiences, e-commerce platforms might provide improved localization and language support.

4. **Ecologically Sound Online Business**
   The concept of sustainability is increasingly being taken into consideration in online business. Sustainable methods and environmentally friendly products are becoming increasingly important to consumers. Businesses that focus on e-commerce may choose to prioritize environmental responsibility in their operations.

5. **Virtual Reality (VR) and Augmented Reality (AR) technologies**

The use of AR and VR technology can create an immersive experience for online purchasing. It is possible for companies to make investments in augmented reality (AR) and virtual reality (VR) applications to improve product presentations and engage customers.

Consumer behavior as well as company practices have been revolutionized as a result of the convergence of e-commerce and digital payment methods. This powerful pair makes it possible for companies of any size to prosper in the digital age by providing an unprecedented level of convenience, efficacy, and global reach.

The advantages of online shopping and making payments digitally far exceed any disadvantages, which may include worries about online safety and the need to comply with various regulations. Because the landscape of e-commerce is constantly shifting, it is essential for businesses that want to maintain their competitive edge and satisfy the ever-evolving requirements of customers in the online marketplace that they take advantage of emerging trends and opportunities.

9.3 Impact of Artificial Intelligence and Machine Learning

Both Artificial Intelligence (AI) and Machine Learning (ML) have recently emerged as potentially game-changing technologies that will have a significant impact on many facets of our everyday life. In recent years, these areas have seen extraordinary developments, which have had the effect of altering industries, increasing productivity, and raising ethical as well as societal problems. During this investigation, we will delve into the influence that AI and ML have had, as well as their applications across a wide range of industries, the obstacles that they bring, and the possible future that they hold within the ever-evolving environment of technology.

A Concise Introduction to AI and ML

1. **Artificial Intelligence, also abbreviated as AI**

   Artificial intelligence (AI) is the process of imitating human intellect in computer programs. It entails the creation of computer systems that are able to carry out activities that would ordinarily need human intellect, including visual perception, speech recognition, decision-making, and problem-solving. AI systems are intended to be flexible, to acquire knowledge through experience, and to carry out tasks independently.

2. **"Machine Learning," often known as "ML"**

ML is a subset of AI that focuses on the creation of algorithms and statistical models that enable computers to learn from and make predictions or judgments based on data. These algorithms and models can be described as "machine learning models." The performance of ML algorithms can be improved over time by recognizing trends and making appropriate adjustments to their behavior.

Influence on a Wide Range of Sectors

1. **Health care services**

   AI and ML are causing a revolution in the healthcare industry by making it possible to detect diseases earlier, provide individualized treatment plans, and improve medical imaging. The ability of machine learning algorithms to examine patient information and diagnostic pictures enables physicians to make diagnoses more quickly and with greater precision.

2. **The economy**

AI is being put to use in the identification of fraudulent activity, algorithmic trading, and the analysis of risks in the financial sector. Models that use machine learning may examine big datasets to spot suspicious patterns, forecast market movements, and evaluate the creditworthiness of individuals and enterprises.

3. **Industrial Production**

Automation in manufacturing that is powered by AI is improving both its efficiency and its quality. Optimization of production processes, detection of errors, and forecasting of the need for equipment maintenance can all be accomplished by robots and machines equipped with machine learning algorithms.

4. **Providing Service to Customers**

As a result of their ability to provide rapid responses and support, chatbots and virtual assistants that are driven by AI are enhancing customer service. These technologies improve the experience that customers have and reduce the amount of human involvement that is required for ordinary questions.

5. **Travel and communication**

AI is playing a crucial role in the development of driverless vehicles, as well as in improving route planning and traffic flow management. The data from sensors and cameras can be processed by machine learning algorithms, which can then make judgments on navigation and safety in real time.

6. **Instruction**

In the field of education, AI and ML are being used to create more tailored learning experiences. Adaptive learning platforms make use of machine learning to personalize instructional material for each student, which increases their level of engagement and ability to retain new information.

7. **Commercialization and Promotional Activities**

Marketing solutions powered by AI make it possible for organizations to study the preferences and behaviors of customers. Using this information, advertising campaigns can be tailored to specific audiences, and personalized suggestions can be produced.

8. **Power and Environmental Viability**

AI is being used to improve the efficiency of energy generation and consumption, as well as to increase the use of renewable energy sources and decrease emissions of greenhouse gases. The ability to predict future energy demand and increase the effectiveness of power grids are both benefits of machine learning.

Obstacles and Causes for Concern

1. **Problems of an Ethical Nature**

The application of artificial intelligence (AI) in decision-making processes, such as hiring or lending, might result in prejudice and bias. It is a huge difficulty to ensure that artificial intelligence systems make decisions that are both fair and ethical.

2. **Protection of Personal Information and Data**

   When it comes to training and analysis, AI and ML rely heavily on massive datasets. The improper use of this data or its improper handling can lead to breaches of privacy as well as security problems.

3. **Being Fired From Your Job**

   There is a possibility that jobs will be lost as a result of automation and technology driven by artificial intelligence. The task of making sure that the workforce is ready for this transformation and able to adapt to new responsibilities is an extremely important one.

4. **Being held responsible**

   When AI systems make decisions that end up causing harm or errors, it can be difficult to ascertain who is responsible for those actions. The development of appropriate legal frameworks for the accountability of AI is a continuing challenge.

5. **Restrictions Inherent in the Technology**

Artificial intelligence and machine learning are only as good as the quality and amount of the data they are taught on. Research is now being conducted in this field with the goal of overcoming these limits and expanding AI's capabilities.

The Prospects for Machine Learning and AI

1. **The Use of AI in Medical Care**

   It is anticipated that AI will continue to make inroads into the healthcare industry, where it will contribute to the drug discovery process, patient monitoring, and individualized treatment programs. The use of telemedicine and diagnostic technologies powered by AI will become increasingly common.

2. **Driverless Cars and Trucks**

   The development of technology for autonomous vehicles will eventually result in transportation networks that are both safer and more efficient. The use of autonomous vehicles, such as cars and trucks, as well as drones, will become increasingly commonplace in the future.

3. **The Use of AI in Teaching**

   More and more people will use personalized learning platforms, which will be supported by AI systems that will provide adaptive educational content and assessments. In the future, educational experiences will also be improved with the help of virtual reality, augmented reality, and other similar technologies.

4. **Intelligent machine ethics**

   Increased efforts will be made to assure ethical artificial intelligence, including justice, openness, and accountability. The development and deployment of artificial intelligence systems will be addressed responsibly by regulation and industry standards.

5. **Artificial Intelligence and Environmental Preservation**
   Artificial intelligence will be essential in tackling environmental concerns such as the management of resources and the impact of climate change. It will be used to maximize the generation of renewable energy, improve efforts to conserve resources, and forecast the occurrence of natural disasters.

6. **Computing on the Quantum Level**

The advent of quantum computing will usher in a new era of advancement in artificial intelligence and machine learning. The advent of quantum computing may one day enable the resolution of difficult problems and the acceleration of the study and training of AI.

Artificial intelligence and machine learning are having a profound and far-reaching impact, having an effect on a wide variety of industries as well as aspects of people's everyday lives. These technologies offer potential and difficulties on a wide range of fronts, from the revolutionization of healthcare and finance to the improvement of customer service and sustainability.

The future of artificial intelligence and machine learning holds the potential of unending expansion and innovation, with an emphasis on ethical concerns and responsible development. The potential for these technologies to improve our environment and find solutions to critical global problems is enormous, despite the fact that problems such as invasion of privacy and job displacement continue to exist. In order to get ready for this future, governments, businesses, academic researchers, and members of society as a whole need to work together in order to maximize the benefits that may be gained from AI and ML while minimizing the dangers that are connected with them.

9.4 Preparing for the Future: Recommendations and Insights

It is essential to embrace proactive measures and be adaptable if we are going to successfully manage the challenges and opportunities that lie ahead as we stand on the brink of a future that is constantly changing. We need to take into consideration the recommendations and insights listed below in order to create a future that is more prosperous, sustainable, and equitable:

1. **Embrace Learning That Never Stops:**
   Because of the rapid pace of change in today's society, it is necessary to continually educate oneself and improve one's skills. To maintain a competitive edge in today's rapidly changing labor market, both individuals and businesses should make education and training a top priority. Participate in online classes, in-person workshops, and professional certification programs in order to broaden your skill set and remain current with developing tendencies.

2. **Encourage creativity as well as collaboration:**
   In the years to come, innovation will be one of the most important factors. Within your organization or community, foster an atmosphere that values creative expression and working together. Create an atmosphere where different points of view are respected and fresh ideas are enthusiastically embraced. Innovative techniques can be developed through collaboration across disciplinary boundaries.

3. **Make the Environment a Top Priority:**
   Concerns about the environment will play an essential role in the future. When it comes to their actions and choices, individuals, businesses, and governments should all put an emphasis on being environmentally responsible. This includes making investments in renewable forms of energy, cutting down on waste, and developing habits of responsible consumerism.

4. **Raise Students' Levels of Digital Literacy:**
   Literacy in digital technology is not a luxury it is a requirement in today's world. It is important for people of all ages to work on improving their digital literacy so that they may more efficiently traverse the digital environment. It is crucial to have a good understanding of technology, internet safety, and personal information protection.

5. **Get ready for the rise of automation:**
   The labor market will continue to undergo profound changes brought on by automation and AI. Creativity, critical thinking, and emotional intelligence are examples of skills that are less likely to be replaced by technology, and individuals should be prepared for the possibility that their jobs will be eliminated by cultivating these abilities.

6. **Maintain an Active and Informed Participation:**
   The globe is rapidly becoming more interdependent on one another. Maintain an awareness of what's going on in the world, what's happening in politics, and what's happening in society. Participate in thought-provoking conversations and contribute to debates that help define the future, whether the topics at hand concern societal concerns, policy decisions, or technical developments.

7. **Encourage an Attitude of Acceptance and Diversity:**
   In a world that is both varied and interdependent, inclusion is an absolute necessity. Acceptance of diversity and fair treatment should permeate all facets of life, including the workplace, educational institutions, and society as a whole. Environments that are more inclusive are better at fostering creativity, innovation, and resilience.

8. **Encourage the Use of Ethical Practices:**
   Both the furthering of technology and the running of businesses ought to be guided by ethical issues. Promote responsible development of artificial intelligence, respect for data privacy, and ethical decision-making across all industries.

Ensure that organizations and governments are held accountable for upholding ethical standards.

9. **Get Ready to Face International Obstacles:**
   Cooperation and preparation on an international scale are necessary in order to address global concerns such as climate change, pandemics, and political tensions. In addition to participating in group efforts to identify answers, you should back public policies and initiatives that attempt to solve these problems.

10. **Foster an Attitude of Resilience:**

The future will definitely bring about a variety of unexpected difficulties. Develop your capacity for resilience by being open to change, retaining a growth mentality, and actively learning from your mistakes. Individuals and groups who possess resilience are better able to overcome challenges and emerge stronger as a result.

The future is full with promise but also holds a great deal of uncertainty. We have the ability to cooperatively build a future that is more equitable, environmentally responsible, and technologically sophisticated if we accept their proposals and insights. As we move forward along this route, the guiding principles that we will use are going to be preparation, adaptability, and a dedication to behaviors that are ethical and responsible.